STANDING IN THE STILLNESS

"Be still and know that I am God;
…I will be exalted in the earth."
Psalm 46:10

Eileen Peters

Copyright © 2009 by Eileen Peters

Standing In The Stillness
by Eileen Peters

Printed in the United States of America

ISBN 9781615791767

All rights reserved solely by the author. The author guarantees all contents are original and do not infringe upon the legal rights of any other person or work. No part of this book may be reproduced in any form without the permission of the author. The views expressed in this book are not necessarily those of the publisher.

Scripture quotations are taken from The *Holy Bible*, New Living Translation. Copyright © 1996. Used by permission of Tyndale House Publishers, Inc., Wheaton, Illinois 60189.

www.xulonpress.com

Forward

One of the greatest wagers of faith is to believe that God's story, written on the tablets of our hearts will bring the deepest stillness to a soul that longs to know Him. If we listen and watch as He writes we will begin to see that His story leads us straight the Father- heart of God. It is not our story after all, but His!! God longs for us to know Him and passionately desires to know us.

"Standing In The Stillness" will entice and invite you to experience the Father's heart as you explore the passion of God, enjoy the provision of God, encounter the purposes of God, experience the promise of God and embrace the presence of God. The finger prints of God are all over every chapter of this little book.

God the Father's story has always been about His PASSION to give us life! He stands waiting to write His story of redemption and forgiveness on our hearts with the very blood of His precious Son, Jesus Christ, in order to adopt us as His own sons and daughters.

God the Father's story is about His PROVISION to meet our greatest need – the need for an intimate, personal and heartfelt experience with our Abba-Father.

God the Father's story is an encounter with His eternal PURPOSE as we accept His invitation to become a part of His big story.

God the Father's story is able to bring stillness to the core of our troubled souls even in the middle of great struggle and loss as we begin to see that His PROMISES are absolutely trustworthy.

God the Father's story sets eternity in our hearts so we understand that the deepest longings of our hearts are merely echoes of our longing for His sweet PRESENCE. These "echoes of Eden" stir our hearts to look for the day when we will see Jesus face to face and hear Him say, "Well done!"

The whole Bible is the story of God's invitation to "BE STILL AND KNOW THAT HE IS GOD." It is the story of men and women who found that invitation irresistible; whose journey to know God became a lifelong adventure. If you find yourself longing for just such an adventure, I would highly recommend "Standing In The Stillness" as a tool to help you on your journey.

Dr. Steve Masterson

Director of Spiritual Formation

Promise Keepers Canada

Acknowledgements

Like guide wires that give stability and security, many people have supported me, prayed for me, believed in me, counseled me, and celebrated with me. They are the reason this book could be written.

My life has been made rich by the lives of fellow travelers who shared their stories and their dreams and allowed me to share mine. Some have walked beside me when my own path became steep and dangerous, and I have felt their hands reaching for me to give me courage.

I am so aware that I have been blessed to have a strong, caring family. I treasure the memory of times when, as a teen-ager, I walked in on my dad as he was on his knees in prayer. I know he spent many hours praying for me. My mom always encouraged me to reach higher than I thought I could and she was always first in line to cheer me on. My grandmother loved me with a love that had no shadows.

To my incredible kids, Shawn and Kristal, and their families, I owe a debt of love that can never be repaid. You have never wavered in your loyalty and enthusiasm for my various "projects."

And to my husband, Lloyd, who has been the wind beneath my wings for thirty-six years, the most precious gift you gave me was to believe in me when I had no faith in my own abilities. This small book is proof of your great love!

My heart echoes the words of A.W. Tozer: "This book is a modest attempt to aid God's hungry children so to find Him. Nothing here is new except in the sense that it is a discovery which my own heart has made of spiritual realities most delightful and wonderful to me. Others before me have gone much farther into these holy mysteries than I have done, but if my fire is not large it is yet real, and there may be those who can light their candle at its flame."[1]

Be still and know that I AM GOD...
Exploring the Passion of God

Be still and know that I AM...
Accepting the Provision of God

Be still and KNOW...
Surrendering to the Purpose of God

Be STILL...
Experiencing the Promise of God

BE...
Embracing the Presence of God

Chapter 1

Be still and know that I AM GOD...

Exploring the Passion of God

"Our pursuit of God is successful just because He is forever seeking to manifest Himself to us."

A.W. Tozer[1]

I don't think there is ever a time that I walk up these steps without remembering that day...

It was the day before the Passover, and the whole city was beginning to throb in anticipation. I too loved the ritual, the symbolism.

I was one of the priests in charge of trimming the lamps on the lamp stand and burning the incense on the incense-altar. I usually looked forward to Passover week, but sometimes I must confess I felt overwhelmed by the relentless repetition of it all. Year after year...sacrifice after sacrifice. Although I didn't want to admit it, deep in my heart I sometimes felt that it was losing importance for me.

Once in awhile I would see someone go by with a young lamb in his arms or a dove in his hands, and I would see in his eyes such a longing to be clean, to feel forgiven. I knew that Jehovah was pleased to accept these sacrifices, but I also knew they could not bring the kind of forgiveness these people were seeking. As much as I loved and respected the ritual, I somehow knew it could not bring anyone to a state of complete justification before a holy God. The old order could never cleanse the conscience of those who worshipped under it.

Those were not the only matters occupying my mind that day, however. It was the Day of Atonement – the one day in all the year that the high priest would pass through the veil and into the Holy of Holies, into the presence of God Himself. On that day he would lay aside his violet robe and its accessories and instead, in vestments of white linen, he would enter the Holy of Holies twice: first to sprinkle the blood of a bullock as a sin offering for himself and his household; then when a goat had been slaughtered for a sin offering for the people he would return to sprinkle the blood once again on the mercy-seat shrouded in a cloud of incense that was burning on the golden altar. It was a solemn but joyful ritual and the focal point of the Jewish tradition of worship.

But on this particular day it was hard to concentrate. I sensed that something was different. The mood of the city was tense rather than festive as it usually was on this holiday, and I went about my duties with a sense of apprehension.

I felt that it had something to do with the impending crucifixion of Jesus of Nazareth, the One who had so infuriated our religious leaders. It was rumored that Pilate was not in favor of His death and was only humoring those who had clamored loudly for it. There were some among us who hoped that Pilate would not suddenly regret his decision and make us pay for it.

Whatever the reason, I felt a sense of disquiet that afternoon. Jesus had been arrested the night before, and it was rumored that before this nightfall our religious leaders would be done with Him once and for all! And indeed, as I moved over the stone floor worn smooth with the sandals of hundreds of priests before me, it seemed to be happening. From where I was standing I could hear the crowd screaming "Crucify Him! Crucify Him!"

I felt a chill in the air as the throng made its way outside the city to the hill of Golgotha. I tried to hurry through my work as the afternoon wore on, wondering what this day would mean for us politically, wondering why this Jesus of Nazareth had insisted that He was the Messiah, knowing all the while He was choosing a course of action that could only spell an untimely death. And I wondered about His ragtag band of followers. I had seen them once or twice – fishermen, a tax-collector... rugged men, but feeling rather vulnerable now, I supposed.

I was moving toward the candlesticks near the Most Holy Place in the temple when suddenly the blackness of night descended upon the land. An instant before, the late afternoon sun had been casting warm shadows over the hills; now there was nothing but thick penetrating darkness. I stood rooted to the spot in terror – and then my heart nearly stopped as I heard a great, rending sound and the thick curtain in front of the Most Holy Place tore open from top to bottom.

I gasped in horror and yet I could not pull my gaze away as the flickering candlelight exposed to my eyes for the first time the holiest place in all the temple – the place where God's presence dwelt!

I knew the penalty for entering into the presence of the Most High God uninvited. I was well aware that no mortal could look upon the face of God and live. And yet that's exactly what I felt I was doing. My mind simply could not comprehend what was happening!

God's holy presence was the centerpiece of the Jewish nation. From childhood the Israelites learned the stories of how God had appeared to Abraham, Isaac, and Jacob to tell them that He was going to make a great nation out of them. Again and again they heard how the almighty Creator-God had chosen to make them His own people and to make Himself known to them. The ancient rituals and traditions that brought the presence of God to them were familiar; the holy days were carefully obeyed. They knew their God was holy.

Each year they celebrated the Passover to commemorate that amazing night when God brought them out of the slavery of Egypt to give them the land He had promised to their ancestors. As they prepared the bread without leaven, poured the wine, and ate their meal together they remembered their deliverance by the hand of Moses.

Moses had appealed to the Pharaoh again and again, they were told, to allow the Israelites to leave. Over and over he had gone with the same message from God, "Let my people go!" But Pharaoh would not listen. His heart was as hard as stone. Finally God told Moses that He was going to send one final plague that would convince Pharaoh to let the people go

– every first-born male in every family and flock in the land of Egypt would die.

But God would save His people, the Israelites, from this terrible judgment if they would follow His direction and sacrifice a young male lamb or goat and sprinkle the blood on the doorframe of their house. The Israelites obeyed and the angel of death passed over them. But in the homes of the Egyptians there was great wailing and weeping, and during the night Pharaoh sent word to Moses begging him to take the Israelites and leave.

Deliverance had finally come, and they began the long journey to the land God had promised to give them. Out into the desert they went, an assorted group of fathers, mothers, children, grandparents, babies, cows, goats, donkeys, pots, bedding, and lots of jewelry. God's people were on the move!

Moses had been leading the children of Israel through the desert for two months when the Lord appeared to them from Mount Sinai. It was an awesome appearance, filled with powerful thunder and lightning and smoke billowing into the sky. The whole mountain shook with a violent earthquake as Moses entered the presence of God on the top of the mountain.

The people stood at the bottom watching with fear. They had been warned upon threat of death not to touch the mountain when the holy presence of God was on it.

And the glorious presence of the Lord rested upon Mount Sinai, and the cloud covered it for six days. On the seventh day the Lord called to Moses from the cloud. The Israelites at the foot of the mountain saw an awesome sight. The awesome glory of the Lord on the mountaintop looked like a devouring fire. Then Moses disappeared into the cloud as he climbed higher up the mountain. He stayed on the mountain forty days and forty nights.

Exodus 24:16ff

Up on that mountain God gave Moses the Ten Commandments along with a list of regulations specifying how they should live. But most important, He gave Moses a detailed description of the place where God would allow His presence to dwell. It would be a tangible expression of a holy, awesome reality that would serve as a meeting place – a "sacred space" – where the children of Israel could come and worship God. In fact it was called the "Tent of Meeting." It would be the place where they would come to be still and know that He was their God.

The very presence of God would reside in the innermost room of this tent on the Ark of the Covenant, 3 ¾ feet long and 2 ¼ feet wide. The ark was to be made of acacia wood and overlaid with pure gold inside and out. Its cover would be pure gold. Two figures of cherubim made of hammered gold were to be placed at the two ends of the ark. This was the place of atonement, the place where the sins of the people were symbolically brought and covered. This was where a holy God would be satisfied. And so the people began to build exactly as Moses was instructed.

After months of labor, with skilled craftsmen using precious metals, the finest woods, and the finest linen with cherubim embroidered in exquisite detail, it was finally ready.

As we come to the last chapter in the book of Exodus the words carry a hush of holiness. It is the first day of the New Year. The people have gathered in silent anticipation, watching Moses' every move as the place where God would dwell was finally being completed. They were His people, and He was coming to live with them!

Moses set the frames into their bases, attached the crossbars, and raised the posts. Then he spread the coverings over the framework and put on the roof layers. Next he put the stone tablets with the terms of the covenant into the ark and brought the ark into the Tabernacle. He set up the inner curtain to shield it from view, just as the Lord had commanded.

After that he arranged all the furniture inside the Tabernacle and began to burn the sweet-smelling incense. He attached the curtain at the entrance of the Tabernacle and offered a burnt offering and a grain offering, just as the Lord had commanded (Exodus 40:1-38, emphasis added):

> *Next he placed the large washbasin between the Tabernacle and the altar. He filled it with water so the priests could use it to wash themselves. Moses and Aaron and Aaron's sons washed their hands and feet in the basin. Whenever they walked past the altar to enter the Tabernacle, they were to stop and wash, just as the Lord had commanded Moses. Then he hung the curtains forming the courtyard around the Tabernacle and the altar. And he set up the curtain at the entrance of the courtyard. So at last Moses finished the work.* **Then the cloud covered the Tabernacle, and the glorious presence of the Lord filled it. Moses was no longer able to enter the Tabernacle because the cloud had settled down over it, and the Tabernacle was filled with the majesty and glory of the Lord.**

A holy God had come down to live with His people. Here was the visible demonstration of the words He would speak through His servant David, "Be still and know that I am God...I will be exalted in the earth."

But not everyone fully appreciated the awesome presence of this God so like and yet so unlike the creatures

He had made. Moses had anointed Aaron and his sons to symbolize the fact that they were set apart to do the work of serving in God's presence. They also had specific instructions governing the ritual of worship, and they clearly understood what was required of them as God's servants. But one day Aaron's sons, Nadab and Abihu, decided to do things their own way.

Leviticus 10:1-2 tells us they disobeyed the Lord by burning before Him a different kind of fire than He had commanded. And God's response to their arrogance and contempt was instant: *"So fire blazed forth from the Lord's presence and burned them up, and they died there before the Lord. Then Moses said to Aaron, 'This is what the Lord meant when he said, I will show Myself holy among those who are near me. I will be glorified before all the people.' And Aaron was silent."*

The presence of God was an awesome place, a comforting place, and a frightening place. It was defined by rituals carried out by priests who had been set apart for the important task of maintaining a relationship with God. Ordinary people were not allowed into the presence of this holy God anytime they chose. Someone else always had to go on your behalf, carry in your sins, and then, while you stood outside shivering with fear, make atonement for those sins by taking the blood of some goat or calf into the Most Holy Place and presenting it on your behalf. You waited until he came back outside and pronounced you forgiven, and then you went away, knowing the ritual would have to be repeated again and again.

Until one amazing day when all of that changed forever. That was the day when Jesus, our High Priest, entered what the writer to the Hebrews calls *"that great, perfect sanctuary in heaven not made by human hands and not part of this created world. Once for all time He took blood into that Most Holy Place, but not the blood of goats and calves. He took his own blood, and with it he secured our salvation forever...Christ offered himself to God as a perfect sacrifice for our sins"* (Hebrews 9:11b-12, 14b).

Because we are human, we sin. The Bible tells us that sin separates us from God. Nothing we could ever do on our own could make us good enough to enter the presence of a holy God whose standard is absolute perfection. Sin's power over us is too great for us to ever be able to find a way to God. *So God came to us.*

John 1:14 tells us that *"the Word [Jesus] became human and lived here on earth among us."* In other words the perfect, sinless Son of God became one with us at the very point of our need in order to deal with sin at the point of its strength. *"(God) sent His own Son in a human body like ours, except that ours are sinful. God destroyed sin's control over us by giving His Son as a sacrifice for our sins"* (Romans 8:3). The power of sin and death is its ability to separate us eternally from God. So Jesus Christ, the perfectly sinless One, came in a human body with flesh and blood to show that He was more powerful than Death.

The writer to the Hebrews explains, *"Because God's children are human beings – made of flesh and blood – Jesus also became flesh and blood by being born in human form. For only as a human being could He die, and only by dying could He break the power of the Devil, who had the power of death. Only in that way could He deliver those who have lived all their lives as slaves to the fear of dying"* (Hebrews 2:14-15).

On that day that Jesus died and the curtain was torn from top to bottom by invisible hands, the old way of doing things was done and a new way had come. *"Under the old covenant, the priest stands before the altar day after day, offering sacrifices that can never take away sins. But our High Priest offered Himself to God as one sacrifice for sins, good for all time. Then He sat down at the place of highest honor at God's right hand. There He waits until His enemies are humbled as a footstool under His feet. For by that one offering he perfected forever all those whom He is making holy...Now when sins have been forgiven, there is no need to offer any more sacrifices...Since we have a great High Priest who rules over God's people, let us go right into the presence of God, with true hearts fully trusting Him. For our evil consciences have been sprinkled with Christ's blood to make us clean, and our bodies have been washed with pure water"* (Hebrews 10:11-13, 21-22).

Jesus went straight into the Most Holy Place in heaven with the only sacrifice that would satisfy a holy God – His own precious blood—and on the basis of that sacrifice He opened the way for us to now come boldly into that Most Holy Place! Our place in God's presence was secured the day Christ presented His blood as atonement for our sinfulness.

After Jesus had been crucified and gone back to heaven, Peter wrote these words, *"He personally carried away our sins in His own body on the cross so we can be dead to sin and live for what is right. You have been healed by His wounds"* (1 Peter 2:24).

The Bible tells us that when we believe in Jesus Christ and accept His sacrifice on our behalf, we are welcome to come into His presence and call Him Father. *"So then, since we have a great High Priest who has entered heaven, Jesus the Son of God, let us hold firmly to what we believe. This High Priest of ours understands our weaknesses, for He faced all of the same testing we do, yet He did not sin. So let us come boldly to the throne of our gracious God. There we will receive His mercy, and we will find grace to help us when we need it most"* (Hebrews 4:14-16).

What does it mean to come boldly into God's presence? Let's say you walk into a bank to withdraw money from your account. You're not exactly sure how much you have in your account. You're hoping it's a little more than five hundred, because you need to withdraw five hundred and ten dollars. You walk into the bank, hand the cashier your signed check, and wait nervously in her presence. The longer it takes for her to sort out the money, the more nervous and uneasy you get. Boldness is the last word to describe your situation.

Now let's imagine another scenario. Your father just happens to own all the oil wells in the Middle East, all the diamond mines in Africa, and all the gold mines everywhere else. His resources are limitless, and he has made it clear that all of his resources are at your disposal. You are full of confidence and boldness because you know that whatever you need to withdraw won't even make a dent in your father's resources. You hand your signed check to the cashier and wait patiently as she fiddles about with pieces of paper and the computer keyboard, making the necessary arrangements to get your money. She may occasionally take a glance at you but you're not bothered. The money is available and you know it. A short delay in getting you the money does nothing to dampen your confidence and boldness.

God invites us to come boldly and confidently into His holy presence on the basis of His mercy and grace. His invitation to know Him overflows with mercy, love, grace, compassion, and joy. His very presence is called the throne of mercy and grace.

Someone has said that "mercy is meaningful only to the degree that we understand what we deserve." What we deserve is death and eternal separation from God. What we are offered is all-inclusive, all-encompassing forgiveness and mercy and grace and an invitation to come freely into His presence.

This is what it means to be a Christian, a "Christ-one." This is the starting point to "Be still and know that He is God." Romans 3:23-25 tells us that *"...all have sinned; all fall short of God's glorious standard. Yet now God in His gracious kindness declares us not guilty. He has done this through Christ Jesus, who has freed us by taking away our sins. For God sent Jesus to take the punishment for our sins and to satisfy God's anger against us. We are made right with God when we believe that Jesus shed His blood, sacrificing His life for us."*

The first step in knowing God always begins with an acknowledgment that we are sinners. We agree with God that we've missed the mark. And the penalty for "missing the mark" is death – eternal separation from God.

It doesn't matter whether our sins are big or small, whether anyone knows about them or not. I once heard someone explain it this way: If a bus is scheduled to leave at 3:10, it really doesn't matter if you get to the bus station at 3:11 or 3:15 or even 5:00. You've missed the bus.

Second, we acknowledge that the only way for us to be welcomed into God's presence is by accepting what Jesus did for us on the cross. It's a free gift, the Bible says. *"For God so loved the world that he gave his only Son, so that everyone who believes in him will not perish but have eternal life"* (John 3:16). Jesus died so we could live.

And when we truly accept this gift of eternal life, we will begin to live in such a way that God's agenda, not ours, becomes the energizing force for everything we do. Ephesians 2:10 tells us that *"we are God's masterpiece. He has created us anew in Christ Jesus, so that we can do the good things He planned for us long ago."* The journey to know God begins with faith, and faith will carry us every step of the way.

This invitation to know God and be known by Him is an amazing journey that sometimes leads us through dark and unfamiliar paths. There will also be times when our steps are strong and sure and we find our days filled with joy. But at all times, whether or not we believe it, our Father is guiding, watching, weeping, and loving. He will never leave us. And we are always welcome in His presence.

Chapter 2

Be still and know that I AM...
Accepting the Provision of God

"To see Jesus is to apprehend Him as the supply of our present needs and believingly to lay hold on Him as such. The Lord Jesus is always seen through the eye of need. He is presented to us in the Scriptures not for our academic contemplation and delight, but for our desperate need as sinners and weaklings."

Roy and Revel Hession[1]

Standing In The Stillness

When our youngest granddaughter was a nursing baby, she developed a habit that was endearing and amusing to see. She would begin nursing with a ferociousness that gradually waned as her little belly filled up. Then, as she began to relax, she would throw her arm outward and move one little leg straight up till her foot was resting on her mother's shoulder. She was completely at rest as she continued to take the nourishing milk. She never thought about the next time she would be hungry. She didn't care if there was a supply in the refrigerator if this one should fail. She just received the comfort and nourishment and didn't worry about the next time.

We are needy people. As human beings we have basic needs that must be met if we are to survive. Even the most self-reliant person would quickly die without sufficient water. And besides our basic needs for food and water and shelter, we have emotional, spiritual, and relational needs.

This reminds me of Bob in the movie *What About Bob?* trying to convince his therapist, who is on vacation, that he (Bob) will not survive without him. When Bob at last gets his therapist on the phone, his words are plaintive: "I need, I need, I need!"

In truth that is the way we should present ourselves before God: "I need, I need, I need!" And often we do; the problem, however, is that we are not thinking of the same things as God. We are saying, "I need this or that to make life work!" And we fail to hear God saying, "I've already given you everything you need. What you really need is to learn to trust Me and take what I offer."

The greatest danger in our neediness is not that we may die but that we may give into the temptation of taking the easy way out. We throw up our hands and say, "This business of trusting God is just too complicated!" We want a quick fix – not a lesson in holy living. And so we try to get water from empty wells.

It seems rather futile to go to a well that is dry and expect to draw water. And yet that's what God said His people were doing when they prayed to idols and asked the king of Egypt for help instead of turning to Him and trusting Him. God told Jeremiah, the prophet, *"My people have done two evil things. They have forsaken Me – the fountain of living water. And they have dug for themselves cracked cisterns that can hold no water at all!"* (Jeremiah 2:13).

The empty wells are all around us and so easily accessible. We go back to a destructive relationship, or give into that habit just one more time, and we breathe a sigh of relief. Or we discover some new strategy to distract us from the pain of an intolerable situation. But in the end the law of diminishing returns that demands more and more to maintain the same level of satisfaction or the same kind of control will eventually destroy us.

On September 13, 1987, in a small city in central Brazil, Wagner Mota, 19, and Roberto Santos Alves, 46, who earned a meager livelihood collecting garbage and doing odd jobs, found a large metal machine in an abandoned cancer clinic. They loaded it into their wooden handcart and took it to a local scrap metal dealer, Ivo Ferreira, who bought it for $30. The men broke open the heavy lead casing with hammers and found a luminous blue powder inside. Santos rubbed it on his right arm to watch it shine; Ferreira gave some to his daughter, Leide, 6, who played with it – and later, with fingers glowing, ate a piece of bread. The group later showed the glowing powder to admiring families and friends. Everyone wanted to see this new discovery. It seemed the men had stumbled onto a way to bring in some quick cash. Eventually, at least 245 people were exposed to the powder. What they did not know was that they were playing with death in the form of a radioactive substance called cesium 137.

Leide and her 37-year-old aunt had died by week's end, while 10 others, including Leide's father, were in critical condition in hospital. The November 2, 1987 issue of Maclean's reported that, "At least 41 other people... were hospitalized suffering from the effects of severe contamination. Bleeding internally, losing their hair and teeth, they are wracked with deep, burning pains and their skin is swollen and blistered. On Oct. 14, Santos's arm was amputated. Many more local residents, doctors say, will eventually develop cancer."[2]

The easy way out is often so enticing and may seem like a quick answer to our need, but God says to us, through the prophet Isaiah, *"The life of your soul is at stake!"* (Isaiah 55:3). Finding satisfaction or sustenance in anything or person or place besides God will surely lead to death.

In stark contrast to the empty wells around us, God gives His people an invitation to come and freely quench the hunger of our souls: *"Is anyone thirsty? Come and drink— even if you have no money! Come, take your choice of wine or milk—it's all free! Why spend your money on food that does not give you strength! Why pay for food that does you no good? Listen and I will tell you where to get food that is good for the soul!"* (Isaiah 55:1-2).

The food that is "good for the soul" is only found in the great I AM. In Psalm 23 David says that because the Lord is our Shepherd, we actually have (already possess) everything we need. Everything we need to answer the heart's deepest longings and quiet all of our fears. When we begin to seek Him as the answer to our deepest longings, we learn to know Him as the great I AM. God our Provider invites us to "Be still and know that I AM."

Have you ever prayed for God to do something for you and seemed to get no response? And then you decided (or someone told you) that if God wasn't answering your prayer, then you must be asking for the wrong thing. So off you went to try to figure out what you really did need, so you could ask for that.

However, the question is not whether God is going to supply our needs. The simple fact is that He has already supplied exactly what we need! The problem lies in our inability to correctly define what we need. *Our deepest need is for God Himself, and He has already given Himself to us.* What we really need is for God to open our eyes to see Him for who He is.

How often have we stewed and fretted about a decision we had to make, instead of listening to Him say, "I AM your wisdom. Come close to Me and you'll find all the wisdom you need to make a decision that glorifies Me."

Or we're afraid, and so we ask God for courage to face tough times, when all along He is saying to us, "I AM your strong tower. I'm already here. You don't need to ask for courage, you need to ask for Me."

Or we may find someone too hard to love, and we pray, "Lord, I just can't love this person," and He whispers, "Why don't you just come close to Me and let My love flow *through* you to that person."

In their book *We Would See Jesus*, published almost fifty years ago, Roy and Revel Hession give a unique perspective on Jesus' words in John 8:58: *"Before Abraham was, I AM."* As they point out, Jesus' statement gets our attention for several reasons. First, it takes liberty with our grammar. If the Lord Jesus had merely wanted to express the fact of His pre-existence, He would have said, "Before Abraham was, I was." But He says, "Before Abraham was, I AM."[3]

What He is doing is taking us back to that day when Moses met God at the burning bush, and asked God what name he should give Him. God's reply was, *"I AM THAT I AM"* (Exodus 3:14-15).

After that, God became known as Jehovah, which comes from the same Hebrew root as I AM and means the same. This was the name God used with His people as He led them and provided for them. He was their covenant-keeping God.

He had brought Himself into a covenant obligation with them. To the Gentile nations He was just "God," but to His chosen people He was always Jehovah, "I AM."

As the Hessions point out, "I AM" is an unfinished sentence. It has no object. I am – what? When we look at the Bible, we see that He is saying, "I AM whatever my people need." The sentence is left blank on purpose so that we can fill in whatever we need.

In fact, "apart from human need, this great name of God goes round and round in a closed circle, 'I am that I am' – which means that God is incomprehensible. But the moment human need and misery present themselves He becomes just what that person needs. The verb has at last an object, the sentence is complete, and God is revealed and known!"[4]

God's name, Jehovah, is really like a blank check. You can fill in just what you need, as each need arises. Do you need peace? Strength? Wisdom?

And even better – it's not we who are asking Him for this privilege but God who is pressing it upon us. In John 16:24 Jesus says to His disciples, *"Ask, using My name, and you will receive, and you will have abundant joy."*

If you've ever watched a child make little rivers in the mud in the springtime, you know that you can have a big puddle of water sitting in one spot, but just take your shovel and dig another area lower than the first and the water will surely find a way to flow into the lowest depth to fill it. "Just…so is Jehovah always seeking out man's need in order to satisfy it. Where there is sorrow, misery, unhappiness, suffering, confusion, folly, oppression, there is the I AM, yearning to turn man's sorrow into (joy) whenever man will let Him. It is not, therefore, the hungry seeking for bread, but the Bread seeking the hungry; not the sad seeking for joy, but rather Joy seeking the sad; not emptiness seeking fullness, but rather Fullness seeking emptiness. And it is not merely that He supplies our need, but He becomes Himself the fulfillment of our need."

He is already supplying our every need because HE IS THE ESSENCE of everything we need. So we must ask ourselves what we are really praying for. What is the deepest yearning and desire of our hearts? And if we are completely honest we may have to admit that what we want most of the time is to feel comfortable and happy, or to have life work the way we feel it should.

As a very young child, our son was somewhat of a miniature perfectionist. He liked to have all his cars and trucks lined up before he went to bed at night. One day he came to me in great distress because he had misplaced one of his little cars. "Let's pray, Mom," he suggested. We sat down together on the bed and asked Jesus to show him where his car was. He waited a moment and then, with a rather forlorn look on his face, he said, "I wish God could talk."

The real question is not whether we are coming with the right request, but what is energizing our prayer? Is our motive a desire to enjoy God's presence and do His will more than anything else? Or is it a desire to make life feel better and work better? Is the real motivation that we want something from God, or do we want God Himself! When we begin to long for God more than anything else, instead of praying, "God, give me love for..." or "Take away my anxiety about..." we will begin to find ourselves praying, "God, give me a deeper awareness of *Yourself* today."

And because the Lord truly is our Shepherd and has given Himself to us, we have all that we need for all of life. We are not coming to Him now for wisdom to help us in certain situations; we are relying on Him to *be* wisdom *in* us. We center ourselves deep in His love and He fights the battle for us. We don't need to beg Him to help us to love the unlovable; we simply rest in His love and allow His love to flow through us.

We open our hearts to Him because He is already there. In all our anxiety, our busyness, our striving to "find" Him, He has already found us. He provides everything we need to live lives that are full and powerful, and richly satisfying.

And many times, instead of removing the painful circumstances, He gives us these wonderful provisions right in the midst of them! *"You prepare a feast for me in the presence of my enemies,"* David says in Psalm 23. That's quite a picture! It's like being invited to a banquet table laden with the choicest cuts of meat, fresh vegetables, sauces, delicious salads, sumptuous desserts – and more. The smells wafting our way make us eagerly anticipate this meal fit for a king. We've been invited into the presence of One who is love and joy and peace and we are free to come to His banqueting table, to enjoy the presence of our Host, to partake of the feast He has prepared! Yes, we can still see our enemies out there. In fact, they're gnashing their teeth as they watch us laugh and eat and drink to our heart's content! They know they have lost their power.

We may still have struggles with people who are hard to love; certain personal challenges may threaten to overwhelm us. Difficult circumstances may not have changed, but we can rest in the fact that what God has provided is exactly what is called for in the midst of these circumstances. Our energies are no longer used up fretting and worrying about things over which we are powerless.

David refers to this in Psalm 3:5-6: *"I lay down and slept, yet I woke up in safety, for the LORD was watching over me. I am not afraid of ten thousand enemies who surround me on every side."* And in Psalm 27:5-6, *"He will place me out of reach on a high rock. Then I will hold my head high, above my enemies who surround me."* And again in Psalm 18:48, *"You hold me safe beyond the reach of my enemies."*

We can rest and be renewed *in the presence of our enemies* as we draw strength from the God who shows Himself as the great I AM. Instead of crying for God to remove our enemies, we thank God that our enemies can never remove us from His unfailing love. Rest is not found in the absence of danger but in the presence of God.

And so we keep our eyes fixed on Jesus, who is our source of strength, love, peace, righteousness, wisdom, courage, and holiness, and we run this race with patience, knowing that because He is the Source, He has already provided exactly what we need. We just have to redefine what our needs really are.

When Jesus spoke the words recorded Matthew 6, He was speaking to people who literally didn't know from day to day where the next meal was coming from. He was speaking to people who knew what it was like to live under a harsh Roman government that extorted taxes from the poor. It was to these people that Jesus said, *"Don't worry about having enough food or drink or clothing. Why be like the pagans who are so deeply concerned about these things? Your heavenly Father already knows all your needs, and He will give you all you need from day to day if you live for Him and make the Kingdom of God your primary concern"* (Matthew 6:31-33). And that's the key; the kingdom of God must be our primary concern. But the cares of this world, the deceitfulness of riches, and the desire for things constantly seek to encroach on the heart of the one who sincerely desires to seek the kingdom of God first.

I take this verse to mean that if we are focused on making God's kingdom our primary concern, then our Father will make our needs His primary concern. And if our heavenly Father is focused on our needs, we certainly don't have to be!

It's not wrong to be concerned about our day-to-day lives, our future plans, our relationships, and the thousands of issues surrounding us and the people we love. But all of those things must take their rightful place in our hearts. Jesus said that wherever our treasure is, that's where our heart and thoughts will be (Matthew 6:21). So if Jesus is our treasure, our thoughts will focus on heaven and our hearts will long for the kingdom of God to become a reality in this world. And everything else will fall into perspective behind that.

If Jesus is not our treasure, we will find ourselves consumed with trying to find happiness and contentment in things that were never meant to fill the deepest longings of our heart. In doing so we will find that we have been mesmerized by the glitter of things that, like a radioactive substance, spell death in the end. And we will lose everything.

"Take no thought for your life...be careful about one thing only," says our Lord, "your relationship to Me." We are needy people, but our greatest need is for God.

Imagine that you are standing in front of a dam that is holding back an ocean of clear, cool, refreshing, life-giving water. You are standing on the other side of the water on ground that is cracked and dry, and your greatest need is for water. Your throat is parched and you fear you might die if you cannot drink. A small trickle of water manages to seep through the dam, but it is only enough to make you realize what is actually on the other side. Just enough to make you long for more.

You do have a spoon in your hand with which you are attempting to break through the clay and cement. True, you don't seem to be making much progress, but it gives you something to do.

Now imagine someone comes to you and says, "Look! There's a huge machine right over there that could break through this dam and allow the life-saving water to flow over you. Why don't you stop trying so hard to break through on your own and let this powerful earth-mover do it for you?"

And now you have a choice. Either you will throw down your spoon and trust the mighty earth-moving equipment to do what it was meant to do so that you can live, or you will stay beside this little trickle of water and eventually die.

"Listen, for the life of your soul is at stake" (Isaiah 55:3). God extends His invitation to us to be still and know that He is the great I AM who stands ready and willing and longing to meet the deepest needs of our heart. He is the ocean of life-giving water that our parched souls so desperately need. But we must make the choice to take the provision.

One of my favorite people is a woman named Acsah. I discovered her many years ago in the book of Joshua. Her father, Caleb, was one of the twelve spies sent by Moses to explore the amazing provision that God prepared for the children of Israel. Along with Joshua, Caleb was a man who saw what the other ten refused to see. The others saw insurmountable problems; Caleb and Joshua saw unbelievable potential for blessing!

Acsah's story is recorded in Joshua 15:13-19. Acsah had acquired some land from her father, but apparently it did not have enough water to make it viable. So she went to her father, Caleb, and said, "You have been kind enough to give me land in the Negev; please give me springs as well." And her father did. In fact, he gave her two springs to water her land.

I'm not sure why that story intrigues me except that I know there have been many times when I sat around bemoaning a lack of resources, fretting over my inability to move forward; crying about the giants instead of taking the resources that were right there in front of me to more than meet my need. I long to be more like Acsah and Caleb and Joshua.

I want to move through life with the blank check firmly in hand, knowing that whatever I need has already been supplied, living as though my Father really does own it all and confident in the knowledge that He is the great I AM!

Chapter 3

Be still and KNOW...

Surrendering to the Purpose of God

"Our relinquishment is a full and wholehearted
agreement with God that His way
is altogether right and good."

Richard Foster[1]

"'For I know the plans I have for you,' says the
LORD, 'plans to prosper you and not to harm you,
plans to give you hope and a future.'"

(Jeremiah 29:11)

We used to live near a beautiful flower shop called The English Gardens. The name always made me think of quiet afternoon tea in a garden filled with beautiful pots of flowers. I loved wandering down the aisles, touching the pretty pots, and admiring the arrangements of plants and flowers. There's something earthy and promising about an earthenware pot. What could I plant in this pot? Where could I set it so that it would complement the other flowers? The pots in The English Gardens were all so unique and beautiful, and they reminded me of the many times God used the image of pottery to teach us important truths.

The creation of a handmade pot is an act of love. The potter already knows what his pot will look like before he starts. He bends over his wheel to mold and shape his lump of clay with hands that are gentle and strong. As his foot controls the spinning wheel, he presses and pulls the clay with his fingers. If it becomes too dry, he dips his hand into the water bowl nearby and brings to the clay exactly what it needs in the process of becoming what it was meant to be. His brow is furrowed in concentration as the vessel begins to take shape. An extra touch here, a dip over there, and the pot is becoming a beautiful object unlike any other the potter has made.

All of this the potter could not do if the clay was not soft and pliable. And this was exactly the picture God was giving His people when He said to them through Isaiah, *"Does a clay pot ever argue with its maker? Does the clay dispute with the one who shapes it, saying, 'Stop, you are doing it wrong!' Does the pot exclaim, 'How clumsy can you be!'"* (Isaiah 45:9). How preposterous to think of the little pot rearing up on its feet right there on the potter's wheel and taking exception to the master's plan! How could it know the purpose for which it was being made? How could it fathom the love of the potter in whose hands it was being shaped?

Everyone wants to live a life that has meaning and purpose. Whole industries have been built trying to help people feel good about themselves. Some people try to find meaning in amassing great wealth. Others choose to find it by becoming famous. Many believe that significance is found in doing good deeds, in serving others. But even so, many people wander through life never really knowing the purpose for which they were created.

"Everything has a purpose," someone says to you. "Things happen for a reason." But sometimes it seems so hard to find that reason, to know that purpose. As a Christian who truly wants to honor God in our day-to-day living, we will at some point likely find ourselves agonizing over the question of God's will in a given situation. Should we do this or that? Go here or there?

God says to us, "Be still and KNOW My purpose for you...know that I AM God; know that My way always brings life and joy and fulfillment." But sometimes we don't listen very well. We're too busy trying to make life work according to our timetable and our agenda. It's hard not to be obsessed with our own comfort and enamored with our own goodness, and when we come to God it is more with a justification about why He should go to work for us and do it quickly than it is about finding what His purpose actually is.

The place to begin is by facing this question: Do I want to know God in order to further His agenda in this world and in my life, or do I want to know Him because it would make my life more manageable and more comfortable? In other words, what is our starting point: our needs and rights and expectations, or God's glory?

In Isaiah 45:4-6 we hear God telling His people that He had a divine purpose for them, *"And why have I called you for this work? It is for the sake of Jacob my servant, Israel my chosen one. I called you by name when you did not know me. I am the LORD; there is no other God. I have prepared you, even though you do not know Me, so all the world from east to west will know there is no other God. I am the LORD, and there is no other."*

God's agenda is always His glory, and He gives us, mere humans, an opportunity to be the vehicle through which the world will know who He is! If only the little pot could know the amazing, wonderful purpose for which it was being made. If only we knew the purpose of the Master as He molds and shapes us. If only we had eyes to see the unimaginably glorious things He means to give us and do through us. If only our finite minds could grasp the wonders of being part of the plan through which God's glory will be shown to the whole earth—a plan that is infinitely bigger than anything we could imagine.

God had told His people He had a divine purpose for them. And yet the Israelites were still stubbornly seeking their own way. They were trusting in horses and chariots instead of the name of the Lord, their God. They were allowing themselves to be seduced and satisfied by the very things their God said He hated!

What does it mean to be pliable in the hands of the Potter? What does it mean to be surrendered to the ultimate purpose of God? What is the will of God for us?

We find the answer in Romans 8:28. What this verse is telling us is that God makes everything work together to accomplish His good purpose for us, and that purpose is clearly stated in verse 29. His ultimate plan is to make us more and more like His Son, Jesus Christ.

The King James Version uses the word "conform" to describe this process. It's a good word. It means to make similar in form, nature, or character. To "conform" implies both an action and a choice. We may be conformed by the actions of someone outside of ourselves, or we may choose to conform ourselves to some pattern or person. A desire to know God that is birthed in the context of total surrender will produce in us a desire to become like Him.

But even though we do want to become like Jesus, and we do want His purpose to be accomplished in our lives, we struggle with the idea of completely giving up all our rights and letting go of our demands to have life work the way we think it should. We fear surrender as though it will mean the end of our very selves and everything we have known. We think of it as something heavy and repressive.

Unfortunately, because we are earthly beings, what we see and feel often has more substance for us than spiritual realities. And that leads us to think of surrender as "away from," rather than "into." We grieve for all the things that might be stripped away, instead of focusing on how we are being drawn ever closer to the heart of the Father! We fear the loss of things we have come to believe give life meaning for us—a habit, an attitude, a possession—rather than believing the promise that Jesus has come not only to give life meaning, but to give us life itself!

In a sense surrender *is* a stripping away—but when at last we let go, we find that what was stripped away was dust and sand compared to the riches that God was waiting to pour into our life. And we begin to see that this is the purpose of God for us—to bring us to that place of complete surrender where Jesus at last becomes more precious than anything else. To bring us to the moment when we cry from the depths of our being, "Make me like You, Jesus!" This is the place where we begin to know with certainty His plan and His purpose for us. And it is only here that we get a glimpse of what it might mean to become the vessel the Potter knew all along He wanted to create.

God's ultimate purpose is to satisfy us deeply. But He cannot do that while we cling to our little toys and trinkets and whimper with fear at the thought of surrender. Richard

Foster says, "God has to help us let go of our tiny vision in order to release the greater good He has in store for us."[2]

Becoming pliable means honoring and obeying God in every area of my life: what I say, what I do, what I allow to entertain me, what I think. Nothing is mine to demand. And I find my flesh shrinking away from that kind of radical surrender. It screams for comfort, it slinks away like a coward. We want to be powerful without paying the price. We want to know Christ but we do not want to suffer with Him. We want what He can give more than we want Him.

This calls for a radically different way of thinking about God's purposes, John Piper defines it as the difference between the biblical mindset and the secular mindset.

> What I mean by the secular mindset is not necessarily a mindset that rules God out or denies in principle that the Bible is true. It's a mindset that begins with man as the basic given reality in the universe. All of its thinking starts with the assumption that man has basic rights and basic needs and basic expectations. Then the secular mind moves out from this center and interprets the world, with man and his rights and needs as the measure of all things.
>
> What the secular mindset sees as problems are seen as problems because of how things fit or don't fit with the center – man and his rights and needs and expectations. And what this mindset sees as successes are seen as successes because they fit with man and his rights and needs and expectations.
>
> This is the mindset we were born with and that our secular society reinforces virtually every hour of the day in our lives... It is so much a part of us that we hardly even know it's there. We just take it for granted – until it collides with another mindset, namely the one in the Bible.

The Biblical mindset is not simply one that includes God somewhere in the universe and says that the Bible is true. The Biblical mindset begins with a radically different starting point, namely, God. God is the basic given reality in the universe. He was there before we were in existence – or before anything was in existence. He is simply the most absolute reality.

And so the Biblical mindset starts with the assumption that God is the center of reality. All thinking starts with the assumption that God has basic rights as the Creator of all things. He has goals that fit with his nature and perfect character. Then the Biblical mindset moves out from this center and interprets the world, with God and his rights and goals as the measure of all things.

What the Biblical mindset sees as basic problems in the universe are usually not the same problems that the secular mindset sees. The reason for this is that what makes a problem is not, first, that something doesn't fit the rights and needs of man, but that it doesn't fit the rights and goals of God. If you start with man and his rights and wants, rather than starting with the Creator and his rights and goals, the problems you see in the universe will be very different.[3]

We are to be still and know that He is God, not in order to get our needs (as we define them) met. God is not a cosmic candy dispenser to whom we come with our wishes and desires to plug in our penny and go away with our candy. We enter His presence only on the basis of what the sinless Son of God has accomplished to glorify His Father, and with the angels we cry, "Holy, Holy, Holy!"

God's agenda is to glorify Himself. We are invited to be still and know that He is God, not for our own benefit but for

His. *"I will be honored by every nation. I will be honored throughout the world."* (Psalm 46:10)

So often we use the words of Psalm 46:10 to meet our needs and desires instead of realizing that it is an invitation to shift our focus from what we think we need and what we think God should do for us to understanding that He invites us to partner with Him in ways that will bring glory to Him and pour into our lives joy and blessing beyond our wildest imagining.

This was the situation Paul described as a "war" in Romans 7. And this is the war I find going on in my own heart sometimes. I want to get right down off the Potter's wheel and have nothing to do with His purpose for me. But that very struggle, in fact, becomes a place that needs to be contoured and shaped a little more, and the Potter knows that. And every time I come to my senses and become pliable in the Potter's hand again, God continues to work in my life. Oswald Chambers has said that surrender means "being united with Jesus in His death until nothing ever appeals to you that did not appeal to Him."[4]

I remember as a very young woman being challenged by a missionary who taught us to pray these words of surrender: "Anything, Anytime, Anywhere." Many years later I am still learning that God's purposes for my life are deeply satisfying and very good.

Amy Carmichael is a woman who has greatly influenced my life. She was born on December 16, 1867, in the village of Millisle, North Ireland. At an early age she fell in love with Christ and gave herself unconditionally to Him. She soon realized that the purposes of God for her would mean not only serving those less fortunate in her own country, but bringing the Good News of salvation to people far away. At the tender age of twenty-six she sailed for China and then on to India where she spent her entire life without a single furlough, until she died on January 18, 1951, at the age of eighty-four.

Amy, or "Amma" as she was lovingly called, was completely surrendered to the will of God for her life. She held nothing back and found that the more she gave, the more God poured into her life and through her to thousands of women and children in India, many whom she snatched from a cruel life as temple prostitutes. She was a prolific writer, and through her writing she continues to influence people all over the world. I often find myself praying her words, and the following poem is one of my favorites.

> Lord crucified, O mark Thy holy Cross
> On motive, preference, all fond desires;
> On that which self in any form inspires,
> Set Thou that Sign of loss.
>
> And when the touch of death is here and there
> Laid on a thing most precious in our eyes,
> Let us not wonder; let us recognize
> The answer to this prayer.[5]

Jesus is the supreme example of surrender to the purposes of the Father. Jesus' first priority was always to bring glory to God. As we study His life we begin to see that in every situation He always acted in complete surrender to His Father. He spent long nights in prayer to learn His Father's will so that He could live and move in total obedience to God.

Sometimes we make God's will something large and confusing. We struggle with "knowing God's will" as if He were hiding it from us. But the purpose of the Father for you and me is to be like Jesus. It's really quite simple and very clear. And it's an all-inclusive invitation.

We had a friend who was a potter. From time to time his travels would bring him to our area and he would stay with us. One morning over breakfast we began talking about his craft. He told us how frustrating it was to get a lump of clay on the wheel and begin spinning the wheel only to find that the clay was not centered. There was absolutely nothing to do, he said, except scrape it off and start again. You might think that with a little adjustment you could fix things, but in the end you would just be wasting your time. The clay must be absolutely centered on the wheel.

There seems to be no middle ground in this matter of surrender either. God does not allow us to decide exactly where we want to be situated on the wheel of His perfect will. We do not have the option of perusing His proposals for our lives so we can decide whether or not we wish to accept. We cannot compartmentalize and say, "I think I'll choose this and this, but not that." God will only satisfy us with Himself, and we will only know Him when we surrender completely to His purpose for us.

Sometimes we wish God would just give us a "divine list of things to do to make God happy." Then we could check things off and feel smug about how much better we were doing than everyone else. But true surrender doesn't work that way. It's not a list of things we must and must not do. It's a new way of living, a new perspective that governs all of life. Oswald Chambers says, "Surrender is not the surrender of the external life, but of the will; when that is done, all is done."[6]

The question we must ask then is: "What do *You* require of me, Lord?" And if God's priority is for us to be like Jesus, the first and most important issue is not whether it's God's will for me to move to another state, or take a different job, or any number of external things that might muddy the waters. The most important issue is a kingdom agenda: whether His glory is the most important consideration for me, and how well I am loving Him and the people and things that He loves.

Standing In The Stillness

It all comes down to this: do we want to count for the kingdom, or are we clutching trinkets and puny possessions that put us off balance and make us lopsided on the Potter's wheel?

Teach me to love Thee as Thine angels love,
One holy passion filling all my frame[7]

We will only be centered on the Potter's wheel as we keep our eyes fixed on Jesus, who brought glory to His Father by surrendering to His will.

Many years ago I learned firsthand how desperately our human nature shies away from surrender. I had been deeply wounded by someone who was very needy. I had tried to love and help this person only to have her turn against me. She refused to try to work things out, choosing instead to bring her grievances to our church community and anyone who would listen. All I could do was stand helplessly by and watch her turn our little church into an uproar.

By the time it was finally over both my husband and I felt battered and bruised, but at least the healing could now begin. All I wanted was to put as much distance as possible between this most painful situation and myself.

I thought all was behind me until one night after a church meeting, I learned that one of the church leaders was concerned that this person, who by this time had left our church with two other families, might have felt that I didn't really love her. (*No kidding!* I thought.) He wondered if I would be willing to find out if this was actually true and apologize to her for any wrong she might have "perceived" that I had done to her.

I was instantly furious. I railed at the thought that after all the months of pure hell she had put our whole church through, anybody could have the nerve to suggest I might have been the offender in any way at all! I felt victimized all over again and couldn't believe that just when healing seemed to be finally happening, someone would be so cruel as to rip open the wound once again. I went to bed, and as I lay there I had imaginary conversations with each of my friends. I pulled out the painful memories and felt sorry for myself all over again. I thought of how indignant people would be when I shared this news with them.

I think I raged and cried for hours, and then suddenly I heard the quiet voice of Jesus telling me that in fact *He* wanted me to do this, not for the church leaders, but for Him! At first I was shocked and then I began to feel that it was so very unfair for God to get involved like this. I knew I had made Him Lord of my life many years before, and I knew deep inside that I never wanted to say no to something He asked of me. And now I was in a quandary. Saying yes to Him would put me in the awkward position of humbling myself before my enemy, and that was one thing I did not want to do. However, as my heart grew quiet and my tears of anger gradually subsided I began to think about Gethsemane. It seemed I could see the lonely figure of the Lord Jesus bent beneath the weight of my sin, praying in anguish to His Father, "Let this cup pass! Nevertheless, not My will, but Thine be done!"

Richard Foster says, "To applaud the will of God, to do the will of God, even to fight for the will of God is not difficult...until it comes at cross-purposes with our will. Then the lines are drawn, the debate begins...."[8]

By the time morning came I was willing to relinquish my demands for "justice" so I could know the purposes of God for me. I had peace, but nothing else. No exuberant joy, no marvelous revelations of glory—just quietness deep within. Acting more out of sheer obedience than anything else, I did what I had been asked to do.

As far as I could tell the situation did not change. But a few weeks later I was walking through the mall with my sister when something struck us as funny. As we were laughing together she suddenly turned to me and said, "This is the first time I've heard you laugh for a very long time!" And I knew in that instant that my obedience, reluctant though it was, had brought healing to the very deepest places of my heart.

"Relinquishment takes us into rugged terrain. The climb is steep, the rocks are sharp, and the trail passes by precarious ridges. From every human viewpoint at times it looks like we have fallen over the precipice to our death. But we know better. We know that we are only falling into the arms of Jesus fully satisfied, fully at rest."[9]

When we take a long look at Jesus we see this: surrender to the will of the Father meant being willing to be broken and pour out His life for those whom His Father loved. And we are called to be like Him.

Paul wrote a letter to the church at Galatia, and in it he gave them an interesting picture of what it means to be like Jesus, to become a fruit-bearer who is controlled by the Holy Spirit. The fruit listed seems very attractive: *"Love, joy, peace, patience, kindness, goodness, faithfulness, gentleness, and self-control"* (Galatians 5:22). We would all like to be known as people who exhibit those characteristics!

And the next verse describes the only way that will occur: *"Those who belong to Christ Jesus have nailed the passions and desires of their sinful nature to his cross and crucified them there"* (Galatians 5:24). That's a shock to our system! The very hardest thing to do is to nail to the cross our "rights," our secret longings, the things that make life comfortable for us. The wood is rough and splintered. Our flesh screams to be taken down. Death is a bloody, painful affair. But apparently we cannot be fruitful and demand that our own agendas be met. Apparently we can't bear fruit if we're only concerned with our own comfort. Apparently surrender really is all-inclusive. As Oswald Chambers says, "Beware of refusing to go to the funeral of your own independence."[10]

But out of death comes life – and life brings fruitfulness. True fruitfulness springs from a passionate, loving union between Christ and His bride. Paul prayed that the church at Ephesus would understand this truth. *"I pray that from (God's) glorious, unlimited resources He will give you mighty inner strength through His Holy Spirit. And I pray that Christ will be more and more at home in your hearts as you trust in Him. May your roots go down deep into the soil of God's marvelous love. And may you have the power to understand, as all God's people should, how wide, how long, how high, and how deep His love really is. May you experience the love of Christ, though it is so great you will never fully understand it. Then you will be filled with the fullness of life and power that comes from God"* (Ephesians 3:16-19)

I have read that during drought conditions and in winter, tree roots travel long distances in search of moisture. As a general rule, tree roots will extend up to 2.5 times the height of the tree, and some species of trees may have roots extending five to seven times the height of the tree. The main purpose of a tree's roots is to capture water and nutrients and to hold the tree in the ground. Roots often find more moisture the deeper they go and so they grow deep into the ground. Paul prays that our roots will go deep into God's love, because that is where the Holy Spirit begins to produce His fruit in us.

Jesus gave the disciples a picture of the vine and the branches to illustrate this. He told them the branches do nothing in themselves; they simply stay connected to the vine and bear fruit! Centered in Christ – deep in His love – that is all we need. Hannah Whitall Smith says, "...In truth, if we only knew it, our chief fitness is in our utter helplessness. His strength is made perfect, not in our strength, but in our weakness. Our strength is only a hindrance."[11]

However, it is never enough for us to simply bear the fruit; that fruit must be crushed if it is to bring nourishment. We are not called to remain beautifully rounded grapes. You cannot drink grapes. We are made to have the life-giving goodness of the fruit squeezed out of us. God's purpose is not to enable self-development. His purpose is to make us like His Son, and the characteristic of Jesus was always self-expenditure. What really counts is not the amount of money you've given to charity, or how regularly you've attended church. It's not even the number of years you've been involved in a certain ministry in your church. What really counts in the economy of God is how the fruitfulness that He produces in you has become life and refreshment to others.

This is so foreign to our Western mindset. We believe in our inalienable right to self-actualization. We want to be self-reliant, we want to be independent, but Jesus calls us to surrender, to crucifixion, to death. Jesus calls us to be like Him.

We can learn a lot from the life of Paul the apostle. Philippians 3 is the testimony of a man who could have paraded his own attributes and gained respect, but instead he gave his own accomplishments the same amount of respect he gave the garbage dump. His focus was completely on Christ and becoming like Him! And so he could say, *"I myself have been crucified with Christ. I myself no longer live, but Christ lives in me. So I live my life in this earthly body by trusting in the Son of God, who loved me and gave himself for me"* (Galatians 2:19-20).

Many years ago my husband and I were in Toronto when we heard that a missionary we had long admired, Dr. Helen Roseveare, was to speak in a nearby church. We decided to go hear her and slipped into one of the back pews shortly before the service began. An older woman dressed in a simple flowered dress sat at the end of the row, and she smiled at us as we said hello. When the service started I remember being surprised to see that the little lady at the end of our row was actually Dr. Roseveare, whom we had come to hear.

I had read her biography and somehow had the impression that this woman who had been so powerfully used by God would have a commanding presence, and perhaps even an intimidating personality, but as she began to speak I realized that her only desire was to reflect the commanding presence of the God to whom she had given her all.

In 1953 Dr. Roseveare sailed for the Congo to serve Christ as a medical missionary with an organization called the Worldwide Evangelization Crusade. The motto of the mission was, "If Christ be God and died for me, then no sacrifice can be too great for me to make for him." And as a young woman, Helen made it her own personal motto.

Because education was a high priority for her father, Helen was sent to a prestigious all-girls school when she was twelve, and after that, Cambridge. She was highly intelligent and very efficient, but at that time single female missionaries were viewed as second-class citizens and that created problems for her.

Finding the medical needs overwhelming, and wanting to make a difference, she dreamed of establishing a training school where Africans could be taught basic nursing skills along with Bible courses so they could go back to their villages to care for routine problems, teach preventive medicine, and serve as lay evangelists. However, she met with disapproval from her colleagues, who felt it would be a waste of time to train nationals to do medical work.

In spite of a lack of encouragement, Helen set to work and within two years she built a combination hospital/training center in Ibambi and her first four students passed their government medical exams.

Just when it seemed her dream to serve Christ in the best possible way was coming true, her colleagues, who were her superiors, dropped a bombshell. Since they still felt she was wasting her time, they ordered her to relocate to Nebobongo to live in an old leprosy camp that had become overgrown by the jungle. She pleaded that she must stay and continue the nursing training, but they insisted she move.

It was a major setback, but she went. She started again from the ground up to build another hospital and continued training African nurses. Still, she was seen as strong-willed and a threat to many of her male colleagues. In 1957, the mission decided to relocate John Harris, a young British doctor, and his wife to Nebobongo to make him Helen's superior. The new doctor even took charge of the Bible class she was teaching. She was devastated. She'd been her own boss for too long, and although she tried to let go of control, she just couldn't. Everything that had been hers was now his. This resulted in tension between them, of course. Her independence was her greatest strength, but also a definite weakness. She did not know how to submit to imperfect leadership. In 1958, after more than a year of struggling over who was in control in Nebobongo, Helen left for England for a furlough. She was disillusioned with missionary work and felt like she might not ever go back to the Congo.

Back in England, she really struggled with the reasons for these issues between herself and the male leaders in the Congo. She convinced herself that her problem was her singleness. What she needed was a doctor-husband to work with her and be on her side during the power struggles! She didn't think that was too much to ask. So she asked God for a husband and told Him she wouldn't go back as a missionary until she was married. She met a young doctor and did everything she could to win his love. He did become her friend but didn't love her enough to marry her. Helen was heartbroken, mostly because she'd wasted so much time and money trying to force her plan into reality—without God.

Still single, Helen returned to the Congo in 1960. It was a tense time for that country, and many missionaries left because the risk was so high, but Helen had no plans of going home. She believed that God had called her and He would protect her. She was joined by a few other single women and was once again given charge of the medical base in Nebobongo because John Harris and his wife left on furlough. She had so many opportunities to minister in the midst of the turmoil and felt she was right where God wanted her to be. She continued to learn to see God in the details of her life, to trust Him more fully. She was learning to surrender every area of her life to the Master.

The rebels were gaining strength, however, and reports circulated of missionaries being attacked. Helen endured a burglary and an attempted poisoning but felt that in spite of the danger the situation was improving. She wanted to stay because there was so much need and so many people depending on her. And then, on August 15, the rebels took control of Nebobongo, and Helen was in captivity for the next five months. On the night of October 29, rebel soldiers overpowered Helen in her little bungalow. She tried to escape, but they found her and dragged her to her feet, struck her over the head and shoulders, flung her to the ground, and kicked her, striking her over and over again. She was pushed back into her house and raped brutally.

It was in the midst of her own suffering that Helen began to see God use her in a way she had never dreamed to minister to other women who had also suffered sexual brutality at the hands of the Simbas. She was able to comfort them and provide a sense of refuge and hope. Finally, on December 31, 1964, she was rescued. Helen had a sense of joy and relief but also a deep sorrow as she began to hear of many people she had come to love who had died a martyr's death.

She returned to Africa for the third time in March 1966. She served for seven more years, but they were years of turmoil and disappointment. The Congo had changed. There was a new spirit of independence and nationalism. There no longer seemed to be any respect for the doctor who'd sacrificed so much for them. In 1973 she left Africa with a broken spirit. Her twenty years of service in Africa seemed to have ended in defeat and discouragement.

When she got home, Helen went through a very lonely period in her life. She turned to God because He was all she had. And as she spent time allowing the Holy Spirit to do His work of healing in her, she sensed that instead of the bitterness and resentment with which she had once struggled, there was a new spirit of humility and a new appreciation for what Jesus had done for her on the cross. God was molding her for her next ministry – one that would, in fact, take her around the world to tell the story of God's grace and mercy. She began to accept invitations to tell the story of her years in the Congo and what God had done in her own life. Eventually she became a much sought-after spokeswoman for Christian missions.[12]

We will never know until we get to heaven how many lives have been touched as a result of one woman who was willing to be poured out and used by the Master. Thousands of young people have been challenged to surrender to the Lordship of Christ because of the testimony of Dr. Roseveare. Many have made the decision to serve God in full-time ministry as a result of hearing her speak.

God is still looking for people who long with all their hearts to know Him and be surrendered to His master plan. He's looking for people who are willing to risk everything for a cause they believe in; people who struggle with failures and fears but refuse to quit. He's looking for people for whom Jesus has become their greatest treasure, people for whom nothing on earth has more appeal than seeing the kingdom of God advance.

God will never force His will on us. He will always give us the option of hanging onto relationships or possessions or dreams of our own choosing. He will let us settle for the good instead of the best. But to those few who will dare to believe with their whole heart that His plan and purpose is altogether good, those who will give themselves without reserve, He will make Himself known. And for them He *"has reserved a priceless inheritance ...kept in heaven... pure and undefiled, beyond the reach of change and decay"* (1 Peters 1:4).

> But I have seen a fiery flame
> Take to his pure and burning heart
> Mere dust of earth, to it impart
> His virtue, till that dust became
> Transparent loveliness of flame.
> O Fire of God, Thou fervent Flame,
> Thy dust of earth in Thee would fall,
> And so be lost beyond recall-
> Transformed by Thee, its very name
> Forgotten in Thine own, O Flame.[13]

Chapter 4

Be STILL...

Experiencing the Promise of God

"The dark night of the soul is one of the ways God brings us into a hush, a stillness so that He may work an inner transformation upon the soul."

Richard Foster [1]

Standing In The Stillness

Have you ever wondered about the beginning of time? What would it have been like to be there when the mighty Word of God split apart the blackness of space and our world—with its galaxies of stars and the sun and moon—was born?

What would you have seen as the twinkling stars were flung from the fingers of God? Or when the sun first rose in splendid majesty?

What would you have felt if you had heard the earth groaning and heaving as the very first mountains were born? Or if you could have been there as the water began cascading down their rugged sides, gathering into rivers that went rushing toward the oceans, pouring into the great depths to fill them up to the shore? Would you have watched with wonder as the tides began to ebb and flow in complete surrender to the commands of the Creator?

And what would you have felt as the breath of God sent the winds to the four corners of the earth to sweep in a mighty force of power...or to whisper through the leaves on a sun-dappled afternoon?

What would it have been like to slide your finger over the velvet petal of the very first flower? Or to hear the very first notes of a songbird?

Do you marvel at the shades of color in an autumn leaf? Or the dazzling symmetry of a snowflake? Have you ever tasted one raindrop on your tongue?

We look at the amazing wonder of the Grand Canyon gouged into the earth by an invisible hand and we're amazed at the power that could do that. We squint our eyes to see the strobe-like fluttering of hummingbird wings and we wonder how such a tiny bird can fly thousands of miles every fall and then back every spring – without getting lost—and our thoughts begin to whirl at this dazzling display of power.

Psalm 19:1-4 says, *"The heavens tell of the glory of God. The skies display His marvelous craftsmanship. Day after day they continue to speak; night after night they make Him known. They speak without a sound or a word; their voice is silent in the skies; yet their message has gone out to all the earth, and their words to all the world."* God the Creator has written into creation itself an invitation to know Him.

The psalmist picks up the theme of God as Creator in Psalm 146:6 and ties it to the promises of God. *"He is the one who made heaven and earth, the sea, and everything in them. He is the one who keeps every promise forever."* The very first name by which God revealed Himself to Adam and Eve was Yahweh, the covenant-keeping God.

God the Creator is the God who keeps His promises. We stand beside an ocean and marvel at a God whose love is deeper and wider than anything we could imagine. Our Creator-God is the faithful Covenant Keeper—powerful, majestic, eternal, and omnipotent.

But here's the problem: sometimes that very same ocean we have stood beside as we gloried in God's faithfulness produces a tidal wave that washes away and destroys everything we've built. Sometimes the gentle wind becomes a raging tornado that sweeps away our dreams. God's promises suddenly seem like a pipe dream without substance, and we become confused. Does He love us or doesn't He? Can we trust Him or not?

Doubt and disillusion become more familiar than trust and courage. Instead of running the race like a strong athlete, we find ourselves shuffling along in despair. Well-meaning friends who are uncomfortable with our confusion rush to give us answers, but their words are like clanging cymbals and we wince with added pain. They urge us to have more faith, but we feel more of a kinship with David's words in Psalm 77 than we do with anybody's faith. *"Is His unfailing love gone forever? Have His promises permanently failed"* or again Psalm 119: *"My eyes are straining to see Your promises come true. When will You comfort me?"*

After a series of unimaginable events reduced Job to a sick, penniless man who sat in the dust grieving the death of his children, Job had a lot of questions for God. But his biggest problem was that he couldn't find God to present his case to Him. *"If only I knew where to find God, I would go to His throne and talk with Him there. I would lay out my case and present my arguments. Then I would listen to His reply and understand what He says to me...I go east, but He is not there. I go west, but I cannot find Him. I do not see Him in the north, for He is hidden. I turn to the south, but I cannot find Him"* (Job 23:3-5, 8-9).

Many of us have felt what Job felt: we try to pray but all we hear is the echo of our own voice in the cavernous darkness. And if we're honest we'll admit there are times when we have even cried in agony, "God, if this is the way Your promises work, I don't want them!" We may feel that we've been stripped bare and left beside the road to die.

At this point we have two choices. Either we quit this journey to know God, or we dig in and echo the words of a man who once said to Jesus, *"Lord, I believe. Help my unbelief!"* (Mark 9:24). And in those words we find the very point where true faith is born, fragile and uncertain though it may be.

It is one thing to go through a painful time of loss or disappointment with a sense of God's loving presence surrounding and guiding us. It is quite another to go through those times with nothing but silence and darkness swirling around us.

We live in a world that is so noisy and so filled with activities and distractions. But if we truly long to know God, He will take us to a place of stillness where He can slowly begin to strip away all the things we have been clinging to. He will knock the props from under us. He will faithfully destroy our false gods. And perhaps the most painful part of the darkness is that it seems to be okay with God when we begin to feel that we can no longer trust Him.

Dan Allender says, "The healing path must pass through the desert or else our healing will be the product of our own will and wisdom. It is in the silence of the desert that we hear our dependence on noise. It is in the poverty of the desert that we see clearly our attachments to the trinkets and baubles we cling to for security and pleasure. The desert shatters the soul's arrogance and leaves body and soul crying out in thirst and hunger. In the desert, we trust God or we die."[2]

This desert place is usually a place where activity seems to come to a standstill. We may feel cut off from things that are familiar, and it is always a place of deep aloneness. And yet the desert is a gift beyond compare given to those whose hearts are just not satisfied to know God on a superficial level.

We come to a sort of crossroads when we realize that what we have called faith was really mostly just fluffy thinking— believing that if we wanted something badly enough and prayed hard enough we would get what we wanted. I think this is one of the things Jesus was trying to teach when He said it would be easier for a camel to get through the eye of a needle than for a rich man to get into heaven. He wasn't saying money was evil; He was saying that when push comes to shove, it's almost impossible for us to resist the temptation to use every resource we possess to try to make life work on our own terms. We desperately want to make sense of what is happening instead of holding onto a God who now seems untrustworthy. But the gift God gives us is a growing awareness that we didn't really trust *Him* – we actually trusted our own strategies. We believed that His blessings as we interpreted them equaled His trustworthiness.

There are many things we think we know about God that we have not actually heard from Him. We've heard them from others or we've heard them through the grid of our neediness, our longings, our pain, our immaturity. The emptiness of the desert exposes the truth about us and the truth about God.

When I was a child I was taught to pray using the acronym ACTS: Adoration, Confession, Thankfulness, and Supplication. I would begin my prayers by running over a few of God's attributes, such as love and holiness – any of the common ones that didn't require too much thinking. Then I would vainly cast about in my mind for some new sins to confess, usually ending up with a generalization like, "Please forgive me for not letting Sara borrow my new pen."

After that I offered a prayer of thankfulness which centered entirely on the good things that had happened to me and my friends. At last I would get to my favorite part: supplication. At this point I would settle into a monologue of requests: "Do this for me, God, and do that for my family and my friends…" and on and on it would go. I always said please and liberally sprinkled my requests with "If it be Thy will," which meant, "I really hope You and I are on the same page, God."

It's hard not to interpret all of God's promises in the light of what they do for us. It's hard not to be obsessed with our own comfort and enamored with our own goodness, feeling that we deserve God's promises *as we have interpreted them*. The quality of our faith becomes apparent when the circumstances of life collide with our perception of who God is.

When life becomes unmanageable, or painful beyond words, it's tempting to launch into a frenzy of activity to "fix" whatever is wrong. But this is the time to be still, to recognize an opportunity to know God in a way we haven't known Him yet. This is the time to wrestle with one of the most frightening questions we could ever ask, "Is God really good, and can I trust Him?"

Real faith is not simply a cry for God to fix things, although we may do that. It is a choice to trust Him even when things don't change, to choose to believe that He is good even though nothing in life seems to bear that out.

A few summers ago we had breakfast with some good friends, John and Andrea, in Toronto. At the end of our meal, John, who at that time pastored a large church in one of the poorer sections of Toronto, gave us a book of three of his sermons. And here's one of the things I found in this little book that flew straight to my heart: "We are mistaken when we think that faith means a lack of doubt. Doubt and faith can coexist. You can have doubts even when you believe."

God's promises do not depend on our faithfulness, or our intelligence, or our power, or even our ability to trust! The guarantee of God's promise does not rest on our ability to understand how and when that promise is going to work out in our lives. God's promises don't even depend on our ability to remain calm and exhibit faith in the midst of the storm.

Not long ago I watched a father in the mall trying to contain the energy of a little boy while his mother shopped. In exasperation the father finally said, "Please stay where I can always see you!"

The only way that would have been possible would be for the child to have remained constantly aware of his father's location. But there were many distractions and much new territory to be explored by a curious little boy. As I watched, I realized that even though the child had been told not to go beyond the gaze of his parent, that daddy was very much aware at all times where his little boy was. Love never let the little boy out of his daddy's sight. The little boy's safety in the end depended on his father's love.

God's promises depend on God Himself. He is the starting place and He is the place where we end. He is our heart's true home, and we echo the song of Moses: *"Lord, through all the generations you have been our home! Before the mountains were created, before you made the earth, and the world, you are God, without beginning or end"* (Psalm 90:1-2).

When Allison Smith lost her big brother in a car accident it was the greatest loss she had ever experienced. Her family was devoutly Catholic and Allison had been taught that Jesus was always with her. "I believed passionately, indiscriminately...If something was connected in some way to Jesus Christ, I was for it."

One afternoon very soon after her brother's death, she says, "I slipped away to the upstairs bathroom to talk to Jesus. As I sat on the hamper alone, Jesus appeared to me; he walked in and sat on the edge of the tub. When I asked him about Roy, Jesus turned his back to me, stood up, and walked away. That was the last time I saw him." And that, Allison writes, was the end of her faith in the goodness of God.[3]

I clearly remember the morning I slipped over the edge and careened down into my own darkness. I felt betrayed and absolutely powerless. A difficult situation had become excruciatingly painful for me, and I felt broken beyond repair. At that moment, and for some time afterward, I truly believed that God did not really care about it.

Sometime later when we decided to leave the ministry, some dear friends made their condo available to us. The condo had a walk-out basement opening onto a wooded area that had been designated as a bird sanctuary.

There was a little cement patio down there, but nothing had been done to develop it so I seized the opportunity to plant flowers, drag rocks into place, and clean out underbrush. It was a kind of retreat in the middle of the city, and we spent many hours sitting in the coolness and listening to the birds or watching squirrels and busy bees.

That little patio area became a place of healing for me, but much more than that, it became the place where I finally came full circle to the realization that if we are to know God, we have to admit there are many things about Him that seem frightening and incomprehensible. What we *do* with the questions that cannot be answered is far more important than finding answers to those questions. If we embrace our doubt and see it as the gift it is, we will realize that faith is not the absence of doubt. It is the decision to trust, even while knowing our questions may never be answered. In the quietness of that little sanctuary I realized that what I *did* know about God was enough to give me the courage to move on in spite of my doubt.

If you have ever crossed a small river on a ferry, you know that the ferry is connected to both sides of the river by a strong cable. You can look from one side of the river to the other and clearly see where the cable is fastened to the shore. However, as you begin the journey across the river you lose sight of the cable as it dips beneath the surface of the water. You don't worry though because you know that even if you can't see it, the cable is there and will hold you fast.

God's goodness and trustworthiness is the cable that holds us fast all through our journey. Sometimes the waters of pain and suffering rise and we can't see the cable, and that is when we need to decide whether we are going to jump overboard or trust what we cannot see.

God had promised Abraham that he would become the father of many nations, and Paul tells us in Romans 4:18-20 that Abraham believed him. God had also said, *"Your descendants will be as numerous as the stars,"* even though such a promise seemed utterly impossible! But Abraham's faith did not weaken, even though he knew he was too old to be a father at the age of one hundred and that Sarah, his wife, had never been able to have children.

Paul goes on to say in this passage, *"Abraham never wavered in believing God's promise. In fact, his faith grew stronger, and in this he brought glory to God."*

But as I read this, I want to say, "Just a minute—wasn't it Abraham who committed adultery with Sarah's maid to try to make God's promises come true? And didn't he show an astounding lack of faith when he said that Sarah was his sister because he was afraid he would be killed if he admitted he was her husband? So how can you say that he never wavered?"

The writer of Hebrews might actually have been thinking about this kind of thing when he wrote these words, *"And since we have a great High Priest, who rules over God's people, let us go right into the presence of God, with true hearts fully trusting Him...Without wavering, let us hold tightly to the hope we say we have, **for God can be trusted to keep his promise**"* (Hebrews 10:21-23, emphasis added). And there's the answer: Abraham did some dumb things and ran ahead of God sometimes, but he never let go of the promise. He never stopped believing that God would make him the father of many nations and bless the world through him.

When God invites us to "Be still and know that I am God," He's inviting us on a journey that is not neat and tidy or predictable. God reveals Himself at the oddest times, it seems, and in the oddest ways. One minute we'll be walking confidently on a path that is joyful and satisfying, when suddenly the ground simply begins to crumble around our feet and we're left clinging to life with no sense of anything stable beneath us. And yet Isaiah tells us, *"If you are walking in darkness, without a ray of light, trust in the LORD and rely on your God"* (Isaiah 50:10). And we cry out, "I thought I was trusting You! What more do you want?"

But God's agenda is entirely different from ours. Ours is usually an attempt to make sure we've stuck close enough to the rules so we can ask Him to give us what we want so that we'll be happy. His is to love us and mold us into the image of His Son so that we will be holy.

This gift of the desert is one we likely would not choose for ourselves. But an amazing thing happens when we make a choice to trust even though we cannot see one step ahead. When we choose to be still in the darkness instead of scrambling toward the light, when we are willing to be silent and quiet instead of demanding to know "why" and "how long," when we are patient though we are quivering with desire for an easy end to our pain, when we choose to be still—we begin to know that He alone is God. *"Be still in the presence of the LORD, and wait patiently for Him to act"* (Psalm 37:7).

Surrender to God's timing and to His agenda brings a realization that somewhere deep in our spirits hope is being born. Faith begins to set the sail and chart the course. Our steps may be tentative and faltering, but gradually we become aware of something under our feet that we did not know was there.

> Nothing before, nothing behind;
> The Steps of faith
> Fall on the seeming void, and find
> The Rock beneath.[4]

Oswald Chambers writes that "Faith must be tried before the reality of faith is actual."[5] In the stillness of the desert we realize that "faith is finally this: resting so utterly in the character of God – that you trust Him even when He seems untrustworthy."[6]

This decision to trust God for who He is regardless of our circumstances becomes a powerful force in the economy of God. We will never understand, until we reach heaven, how the weakest child of God who whispers, "Lord, I will trust You," can literally change the landscape. "God is attracted to weakness. He can't resist those who humbly and honestly admit how desperately they need Him. Our weakness, in fact, makes room for His power."[7]

Standing In The Stillness

The apostle Paul had been given a vision and revelation in which he heard things that were so astounding they could not be expressed. And then he says that in order to keep him from getting proud about what had happened to him, he was given a thorn in his flesh, a messenger from Satan. There has been a lot of speculation as to what this thorn was, but one thing we do know: Paul asked three times for it to be removed. In fact, Scripture tells us that he "begged" to be free of it. And each time the Lord said, *"My gracious favor is all you need. My power works best in your weakness."*

It took awhile, but Paul finally got what God was saying to him: "This thorn is the vehicle through which my power will be seen by a watching world. As you accept this weakness, the power of Christ will become real in your life!" And Paul's response was to say, "If this weakness will glorify Christ, then bring it on!" *"So now I am glad to boast about my weaknesses, so that the power of Christ may work through (rest upon) me. Since I know it is all for Christ's good, I am quite content with my weaknesses and with insults, hardships, persecutions, and calamities. For when I am weak, then I am strong"* (2 Corinthians 12:8-10).

The phrase that is used to describe the power of God resting on Paul here is the same phrase used in Exodus 40:34 when the presence of the Lord came down to live with His people. *"Then the cloud covered the Tabernacle, and the glorious presence of the LORD filled it."* In other words, Paul recognized that just as the shekinah glory came to dwell among God's people, so his life would become a place where God's glory could be seen. God's power rests on us and His glory shines in our lives as we learn to trust Him and become all He has intended for us.

One truth we can hold with confidence is this: nothing is wasted in God's economy. Not one tear, not one trial, not one heartache is wasted. Sometimes we understand God's purposes and sometimes they remain a mystery, but "We can be assured of this: God, who knows all and sees all, will set all things straight in the end. Even better, He will dry every tear. In the meantime He mysteriously takes our sorrows and uses them to heal the world."[8]

One thing is sure. We emerge from the desert changed. My sister sent me an email a few years ago that I pasted into my journal so I could think about her words: "I was thinking tonight on my way to the office that it is far better to have a crisis of faith (and meet it with integrity) than it is to simply let one's faith degenerate into nothing more than a habit. I always think of Jacob, who walked with a limp ever after wrestling with God..."

The story of Jacob has some strange twists. In Genesis 32 we read that after 20 years of working for his father-in-law, Laban, and having his wages reduced ten times, Jacob had secretly left with his wives and children, flocks and servants. He was preparing to cross the Jabbok River, and he knew his brother Esau would be waiting for him on the other side with a 20-year-old score to settle. So he sent an elaborate gift of 550 animals led by servants who were to present them to Esau with some gracious words. Hopefully this would soften Esau's heart. Then he sent his wives and children and all of his possessions over the Jabbok River.

I wonder if Jacob, the schemer, had lost sight of hope. Jacob was a man committed to winning. He could wait for what he wanted, biding his time with the cunning of an animal stalking its prey. He had struggled with his brother and his father-in-law, and he had won. But now he was all alone in his camp. His wives and possessions and (he thought) an angry brother with murder on his mind were all on the other side. No comfort food, no companionship, nobody to talk to. If his plan didn't work out, he had nothing to fall back on.

I wonder if he thought about the promise God had made to him not only to bless him but to bless all the nations of the world. We don't know what thoughts were going through his mind as he sat alone in the darkness, but we do know he was afraid – afraid that Esau would attack and kill him and his family, and that would be the end of Jacob and the end of the promise.

And then suddenly in the darkness God jumps him. If he was afraid before, I think it's safe to say he was terrified now! Genesis 32:24-31 gives us the account:

> *This left Jacob all alone in the camp, and a man came and wrestled with him until dawn. When the man saw that he couldn't win the match, he struck Jacob's hip and knocked it out of joint at the socket. Then the man said, "Let me go, for it is dawn." But Jacob panted, "I will not let you go unless you bless me." "What is your name?" the man asked. He replied, "Jacob." "Your name will no longer be Jacob," the man told him. "It is now Israel, because you have struggled with both God and men and have won." "What is your name?" Jacob asked him. "Why do you ask?" the man replied. Then he blessed Jacob there. Jacob named the place Peniel—"face of God"—for he said, "I have seen God face to face, yet my life has been spared." The sun rose as he left Peniel, and he was limping because of his hip."*

This is a strange story, and there are many things we don't understand. For a few hours during the deepest part of the night, God allows the invisible world to touch Jacob's visible world. Sweaty, dusty bodies roll and grasp and thud. The only sound is grunting and gasping until the man touches Jacob's hip and knocks it out of joint. And then the first words we hear are from the man, *"Let me go for it is dawn."*

Jacob was aware that although he had struggled before, first with his brother and then with his father-in-law, this time the struggle was different. This time he knew he had been in mortal combat with the Promise Giver Himself, and as God said to him "What is your name?" he realized that the promise was intact, not because he had been able to scheme and connive, but because the promise had never depended on his schemes, but on God's powerful faithfulness.

As dawn broke over the river hills, Jacob was aware that he had never tasted life so deeply. He had never been so alive. Up to this moment life had been an endless struggle of deceit and trickery. Now he had been broken and made whole. His name had been changed and he had been marked by God. His limp would forever tell the story of a God who always keeps His promises.

I wonder what it would have been like to carry the mark of God for the rest of his life. A friend would say, "Jacob, why are you limping?" And Jacob would shake his head and say, "You never know what God will do when you meet Him face-to-face!"

Life can be either a humdrum experience of seventy to eighty years of going through the motions of living, or it can be a journey of hope that takes us to places that are breathtaking and terrifying beyond compare.

If we're willing to endure the darkness, a day will come when the horizon begins to gray with the dawning daylight. "Although everyone's dark night is different, everyone's way out of the darkness is the same. The only way out of the darkness of night is the coming of the dawn, which is the hope of all who have faced their worst fears in the night."[9]

"Now we see things imperfectly as in a poor mirror, but then we will see everything with perfect clarity. All that I know now is partial and incomplete, but then I will know everything completely, just as God knows me now" (1 Corinthians 13:12).

And what we will know with no more doubt is that God can be trusted.

> God answers prayer. Sometimes when hearts are weak
> He gives the very gifts they seek.
> But often faith must learn a deeper rest,
> And trust God's silence when He does not speak.[10]

Chapter 5

BE...
Embracing the Presence of God

"The feeling remains that God is on the journey, too"

Teresa of Avila

Standing In The Stillness

I will always remember two things my dad taught me. One was that it always pays to serve Jesus. The other was that if you eat chicken wings you can fly. I remember one day as a little girl with my nose pressed against the window pane, watching my dad as he prepared to make good on his proclamation after a dinner of roast chicken. He climbed onto a barrel outside, flapped his arms, cackled his best imitation of a chicken, and jumped off.

The other thing I remember my dad teaching me, he taught by example. I don't remember him ever telling me in words that it always pays to serve Jesus, but I knew he loved His Savior dearly, and that love was the compelling force for everything he did. And he loved the people he had been called to serve.

Dad had made the decision to follow Jesus as a young boy, but his decision was not welcome in the community where he lived. He was so ridiculed that he finally made up his mind that it was impossible for him to continue to be a Christian. He told us how he had decided he would go into the grain field behind the straw stack to pray his last prayer and then go back to his old life.

Instead, as he lay face down in the grain field, he suddenly sensed the overwhelming presence of a loving Father who had already taken note of an utterly discouraged little boy. He later wrote that it came "sweeping over him like strong rolling billows," and in a loud voice he cried, "I will never, never, never, ever go back!"

My dad was not a perfect man. Sometimes he was moody, and I realize now that he struggled with depression. But one thing that everyone knew about my father was that he loved his Lord and eagerly anticipated the day he would see Him face-to-face. Heaven was very real to my dad, and he loved to sing old hymns and gospel songs that talked about it.

As a young man he had been severely injured in an accident and slipped into a coma. He recovered completely, but he used to tell me that at one point while he was unconscious, he began to hear wonderful music, and he sensed a place that was so warm and bright and inviting, and he had a great longing to go there.

Another time he was looking out the window in the early morning at a sky that was spectacular with color. As the sun began to lift in majesty above the horizon, he suddenly felt like he was looking straight into heaven. It was such an "other world" experience it stayed with him the rest of the day.

"When God wants to carry a point with His children," Emerson said, "He plants His argument into the instincts. Our deepest instinct is heaven. Heaven is the ache in our bones, the splinter in our heart. Like the whisper of faraway waves we hear crashing in the whorls of a conch shell, the music of heaven echoes, faint, elusive, haunting, beneath and within our daily routines."[2]

There were other times that became "thin places" for my dad. But toward the end of his life (although we did not realize at the time that it was the end) he began to live with greater anticipation of his home-going. He had attended the graveside service of a friend where everyone was given helium-filled balloons to release as the coffin was lowered. The symbolism thrilled him and he decided that he wanted the same thing done at his funeral. He reminded us over and over again to make sure we wouldn't forget.

Dad would phone me once in a while and say, "Guess what I'm doing. I'm working on my obituary." It was never a morbid conversation. He would read what he'd written and ask for my input. It simply felt more like a conversation with someone getting his papers in order for an eagerly anticipated visit to another country.

Near the end, however, Dad began to experience hallucinations. Sometimes they were funny such as when he told us he had thought men were outside his window cutting the tops off all the trees. Sometimes he would laugh wryly as he told us how he had carried on great conversations with us only to realize later that we were not there. But there was one thing that gave us pause. My father would at times hear music that was so beautiful he would become completely overwhelmed. He would tell us later about the songs he had heard, and we all wondered if he was literally beginning to hear the music of heaven. One time, he said, he was so overcome by the beauty of what he heard that he got up from his chair, went to his bedroom, and knelt in worship as tears streamed down his cheeks.

On the night he died, his covers were folded back as though he had intended to get out of bed. When my stepmother found him he was lying on his back on the floor where he had fallen. I will always wonder if that time, when he heard the music and felt the presence of his Savior so near, he said to the angels, "This time you're not leaving without me!" As his human body fell away that night I believe his spirit was taken up on angels' wings into the presence of the One he had loved and served all his life.

Buried in the highlands of Scotland is a forested valley called Balquhidder. In the springtime the hills are bright with daffodils and the luscious green of new growth. Here the Kirkton Burn comes tumbling down from the hills to join a river whose banks are carpeted with snowdrops.

In the ninth century, a monk named St. Angus glimpsed this lush, meandering depression in the earth. Overwhelmed by its breathtaking beauty and dramatic landscape, he declared it "a thin place" – a place where the separation between this world and the next was almost transparent.

In a spiritual sense we sometimes come quite unexpectedly upon thin places – times when, like warm air on a frosty pane, the veil between what is temporal and what is real is lifted for an instant, and we see that what our hearts truly long for lies on the other side where God's presence will be reality.

In the 1800s a man named George Müller was used by God to care for and educate more than 23,000 orphans in England. He never made requests for financial support, nor did he ever go into debt. He simply believed in the promises of a God who said He would provide. Many times he received unsolicited food donations only hours before they were needed to feed the children.

I have an old book on the life of George Müller that was published around 1899 shortly after he died. One of the most precious things in this book is the description of his address at the funeral of his second wife. He was an old man of ninety, and as he stood there people were deeply moved to see that the faith which had sustained him through many trials was holding him, as it were, on everlasting arms.

This is how that moment, a thin place, was described by one who was present: "He lived in such habitual communion with the unseen world, and walked in such uninterrupted fellowship with the unseen God, *that the exchange of worlds became too real for him to mourn for those who had made it, or to murmur at the infinite Love that numbers our days.*"[3]

George Müller had learned to live with an awareness of the presence of God that enabled him to see Christ in *every* experience in life or death. It sustained him, guided his decisions, influenced his choices, and gave him a heart that longed for heaven.

In the end, what makes our Christian faith different from every other religion? It is the hope that is grounded in the finished work of Christ on Calvary that someday we will be ushered into the physical presence of God. Home at last! With Him for eternity!

The book of Luke tells the story of two of Jesus' followers who had just left Jerusalem after the crucifixion of Jesus. As they were discussing the events that had left them shattered, a stranger came along and joined them. Although they didn't know it was Jesus, they felt strangely warmed as He visited with them and explained many things from the Scriptures. We're told that they invited Him home with them for the night, and when they sat down to break bread together they suddenly recognized that it was really their Lord who had been walking with them. And then He disappeared.

Their joy knew no bounds, and within the hour they were on their way, seven miles back to Jerusalem, to tell the disciples and other friends of Jesus what they had just experienced.

I have always loved the way Dr. Luke, who was there that night, tells what happened next: *"Then the two from Emmaus told their story of how Jesus had appeared to them as they were walking along the road and how they had recognized Him as He was breaking the bread.* **And just as they were telling about it, Jesus Himself was suddenly standing there among them. He said, 'Peace be with you'"** (Luke 24:36, emphasis added).

Sometimes I wonder what it would be like to suddenly look up from what I'm doing – and see Jesus standing there! I can't even imagine how I would feel knowing I was seeing for the first time my precious Savior, who loves me and died for me.

That's what will happen one day when the NOW is gone and the SOMEDAY becomes reality. That's when we'll know we are home.

The beloved "faith chapter" in the book of Hebrews contains the stories of Enoch, Noah, Abraham, Isaac, Jacob, Moses, and a host of unnamed heroes who *"died without receiving what God had promised them, but they saw it all from a distance and welcomed the promises of God. They agreed that they were foreigners and nomads here on earth. And obviously people who talk like that are looking forward to a country they can call their own...They were looking for a better place, a heavenly homeland"* (Hebrews 11:13-16).

These were men and women who had learned how to live in this world even while they were looking for a better place. Every earthly experience was shaped and colored by the realities of heaven and the hope of glory that awaited them. They had learned to know God over a lifetime mixed with joys and sorrows, and they had a different perspective – perhaps not so much "different" as "enlarged." They saw the NOW and were very much present in it, but the NOW was somehow less important than the SOMEDAY.

It's very hard not to become so absorbed with living here that we forget that this world is not really home. We fall into the habit of living as though we have nowhere else to go. But the truth is that we're citizens of another country, called to live in the tension between the glory and the groaning that Paul described. Tension can be a good thing. A tennis racket must be strung with just the right amount of tension so you can control the ball. Windsurfers must keep the right tension in the ropes that hold the sails. A violin string with just the right amount of tension produces beautiful music. And we must learn to balance the living we do NOW with the glorious hope that awaits us SOMEDAY.

To the church in Corinth Paul wrote tender words of hope in the face of constant hardship. Faith in what was to come, he told them, would carry them through.

That is why we never give up. Though our bodies are dying, our spirits are being renewed every day. For our present troubles are quite small and won't last very long. Yet they produce for us an immeasurably great glory that will last forever! So we don't look at the troubles we can see right now; rather we look forward to what we have not yet seen. For the troubles we see will soon be over, but the joys to come will last forever. For we know that when this earthly tent we live in is taken down – when we die and leave these bodies – we will have a home in heaven, an eternal body made for us by God Himself and not by human hands... Our dying bodies make us groan and sigh...We want to slip into our new bodies so that these dying bodies will be swallowed up by everlasting life. God Himself has prepared us for this, and as a guarantee He has given us His Holy Spirit. So we are always confident, even though we know that as long as we live in these bodies we are not at home with the Lord. That is why we live by believing and not by seeing. (2 Corinthians 5:1-7)

Learning how to live HERE when we long to be THERE is perhaps the most difficult part of the journey. But in truth, the more we long to be home, the better we live down here.

The NOW becomes less complicated and somehow more manageable as the sweet anticipation of SOMEDAY comes more into focus. What matters to our Father begins to matter to us as we learn what it means to live in His presence.

All we can see now is the faint outline ahead of something so beautiful that just to imagine it takes our breath away. All we can hear along the path are snatches of music, fluttering of wings, and we know that although "now we see through a glass darkly," at the end of this journey we will see face-to-face this God whose name, said the prophet Isaiah, will be the hope of all the world. And that tension makes us alive – stirs something deep inside, a desire to *be*, to taste life as deeply as it can be tasted.

Philip Yancey tells the story of Robin Graham who was the youngest person in history to sail around the world alone.

Robin set sail as an immature sixteen-year old, not so much seeking his future as delaying it. In the course of the long voyage, he was smashed broadside by a violent ocean storm, had his mast snapped in two by a rogue wave, and barely missed annihilation by a waterspout. He went through such despair in the Doldrums, a windless, currentless portion of the ocean near the Equator, that he emptied a can of kerosene in his boat, struck a match, and jumped overboard. (A sudden gust of wind soon caused him to change his mind and he jumped back in to extinguish the blaze and continue the voyage.)

After five years, Robin sailed into the Los Angeles harbor to be greeted by boats, banners, crowds, reporters, honking cars, and blasts from steam whistles. The joy of that moment was on a different level from any other experience he had known. He could never have felt those emotions returning from a pleasure outing off the coast of California. The agony of his round-the-world trip had made possible the exultation of his triumphant return. [4]

After the groaning comes the glory. Paul tells us in Romans 8,

All creation anticipates the day when it will join God's children in glorious freedom from death and decay. For we know that all creation has been groaning as in the pains of childbirth right up to the present time. And even we Christians, although we have the Holy Spirit within us as a foretaste of future glory, also groan to be released from pain and suffering. We, too, wait anxiously for that day when God will give us our full rights as His children including the new bodies He has promised us. Now that we are saved, we eagerly look forward to this freedom. For if you already have something, you don't need to hope for it. But if we look forward to something we don't have yet, we must wait patiently and confidently.

Romans 8:18-25

A longing to really know God produces the ability to live by the truth that someday our groans will be swallowed up in glory. And that gives us joy and courage and hope. Not the hope that life will be fair, our children will never be hurt, we will never be passed over for a promotion, and earthquakes will not happen where we live. It is the hope that although this journey is a dimly lit path with patches of glorious sunlight streaming in from time to time, this is not all there is; this is not reality.

Learning to live in the tension between the groaning and the glory requires a moment-by-moment kind of living. It means we will realize that the presence of Jesus is not experienced in what happened to us yesterday, or what we're planning for tomorrow. The presence of Jesus is found in the NOW. Each moment is pregnant with an invitation to live life to the full. To experience the abundant joy Jesus came to give us.

Being aware and paying attention to the presence of God is crucial to living as a Christ follower because the degree to which we are able to be fully present in the moment is the degree to which we will be aware of how we are loved by God. And as Brennan Manning says, "You will trust Him to the degree that you know you are loved by Him."[5]

Mary was a girl who knew how to savor the presence of Jesus. She and her sister, Martha, and their brother, Lazarus, had welcomed Jesus into their home many times. On one particular day Jesus and His disciples were on their way to Jerusalem, and Jesus decided to stop in Bethany for a visit with His friends. Martha was undoubtedly a splendid hostess, and she immediately rose to the occasion and began preparing a big meal for them. It was hot in her kitchen, but this was a labor of love.

Mary, on the other hand, had elbowed her way right past all of the big, burly disciples and was sitting at Jesus' feet, listening to Him teach. I always imagine Mary as a vivacious young woman with sparkling eyes and long dark hair, and I'm not sure the disciples appreciated her being right there in that coveted spot in front of Jesus. Likely some of them agreed with Martha that Mary should be in the kitchen. But Mary was living in the moment. She was focused on Jesus, savoring the experience of His love, listening to His voice, feeling the reality of being alive in His presence.

We long to be that free – like a child dancing in the sunshine, oblivious to the cares of this world—but it seems that every time we think we might be making some progress in learning to know God, life brings us back to reality with a thud. A phone call from an aging parent, a boss who is unreasonable, a spouse who is impatient, kids who are demanding, runny noses to wipe.

Living with the awareness of the presence of God simply means developing an awareness of what is true – you *are* in His presence. I love the story about G.K. Chesterton, the great English journalist. As I remember it, he and a friend were walking down a street in London one day when his friend said to him, "G.K., what would you do if you turned around and discovered that Jesus was right behind you?" Without missing a beat, Chesterton replied, "He is."

The truth is that we are always in His presence. Everything we do, everything we say, everything we think, we do and say and think in God's presence! Paul said, *"In Him we live, and move, and exist"* (Acts 17:28).

But living with an *awareness* of that presence means being alive to the fact that there is a spiritual dimension at work in this moment and allowing His presence to comfort, direct, and empower us. It means allowing the presence of Jesus to be our center and our focus. You could call it "present-moment living."

But here's where the rub comes. Learning to be aware of the presence of God is simple, but it is not easy. This business of living in the moment or "practicing the presence of God" sometimes seems like a futile exercise that leaves us frustrated and makes us want to go off to find something more concrete and entertaining. The temptation is to be satisfied with the kind of faith that takes us to church on Sunday morning and leaves us alone the rest of the week.

Instead of living in the NOW we are so often pulled back into the past. Shame so often steals from us the joy of knowing God by throwing memories at us that would be better left forgotten. Words we've said, things we've done, choices we made in a split second that should have been more carefully considered. We play these things over and over in our minds and find nothing to redeem ourselves.

Sometimes anger comes along and reminds us of an unkind remark made in an offhand manner by someone we thought loved us, a slight that we cannot forget, times when we were taken for granted. Soon we realize that all of our energy has been given to the bondage of living in the past, and our present moments have slipped away without us being aware of the joy and beauty that could have been ours if we had recognized the presence of Jesus and His call to live out our lives in the fullness of His presence.

Or anxiety suddenly shoots at us out of nowhere, and we become bound to the future, planning for what might happen, worrying about what we cannot control, and agonizing over what very likely will never come to pass. Brennan Manning says, "More often than not, I do not hear the music of what is happening now because my mind ricochets between the past and the future."[6]

Sometimes we find busyness distracting us. We may even be busy with God's work. Martha was, and she missed the moment. Present-moment living is very hard for busy people. And even though we may know we're allowing meaningless things to distract us, we just can't seem to get off the treadmill. The culture in which we live has engrained in us that *doing* is more valuable than *being!* And so instead of living with a conscious reality that the presence and power of Christ is actually with us in this moment in the person of the Holy Spirit, our souls become chipped and ragged. We long to find rest, but it always seems to be for someone else. We're too anxious inside, too frazzled to be quiet long enough for our own wounds to heal, and often we find ourselves trying to give to others what we are not experiencing ourselves. It may seem to others that we are performing well, but in reality we may have become so inundated with tasks and deadlines and life that we have lost touch with ourselves and with that Voice that calls us to Himself. We have become preoccupied with the trivial, and our preoccupation has become a bandage that keeps us from having to admit that we are actually wounded and not working well at all. We're afraid to face the reality of our brokenness because we think our brokenness makes us unacceptable. We become overwhelmed with the "groaning" and lose sight of the "glory."

Someone has said that hearing the voice of God requires that every other voice within us be silenced. Perhaps the hardest place to find silence is in our own souls. It seems almost impossible to find quiet places in our noisy world. How often we pass right by "thin places" never knowing they were there. But becoming still so that we can experience the presence of God *is* possible. We *can* learn to live in the moment. All it takes is a change of perspective. We try so hard to be still and find it doesn't work. We are so conscious of our own failures and we feel like giving up.

It's hard not to make this sound like a cliché, but the truth is that this kind of present-moment living will become a reality for us as we learn to trust that *all that needs to be done has already been done for us.* Our part is to accept it. We so often think we need to muster up some kind of spiritual desire, some kind of mystical awareness. Really what we need to do is acknowledge that the presence of Jesus is here. Now. Christ has already secured our access to His presence, and the ministry of the Holy Spirit is to make us aware of that presence. "Be still and know that I am God," He says to us. "Cease striving, be silent. Bring the ragged pieces, the broken shards into My presence instead of struggling to keep your brokenness out of sight! Only My presence and My love can heal those broken, tired places." It's a change of perspective – turning our eyes up instead of being chained to life around us.

Sometimes we are given the gift of quietness for a few moments or a few hours. But most often we must learn to find that inner stillness in the midst of whatever is happening. And it can happen.

It can happen in a mother's heart as she's making a snack for her little ones and she realizes the presence of Jesus transforms her kitchen into a throne room where she can experience two or three minutes of conversation with Christ.

It can happen in the heart of a teacher who looks at his classroom full of noisy children and, for a few seconds, slips away into that place of silence to ask for wisdom as he guides those precious lives.

It can happen in the workplace when an employee makes a hard decision that is empowered by a wordless moment of fellowship with the Father.

It can happen as we're waiting in a restaurant and hear God's Spirit gently nudge us to pray for the couple at the next table.

It can happen as we begin to see that ragged drunk through the eyes of Jesus.

It will happen over and over again as we learn the truth that God is found in this very minute. As we begin to live as though that were true, we will find we are truly experiencing His presence in a way that gives us strength and helps us to minister to a world that is broken and in despair. The tension will produce beautiful music.

I was riding on a commuter train in Calgary one summer afternoon when a young man got on and moved to a place a few seats in front of me facing in my direction. He was dressed all in black and had a spiked collar around his throat. His hair was sprayed and spiked and his arms were covered with tattoos and leather bracelets. The thing that really caught my attention, however, were the words on his T-shirt: "I AM SATAN." I looked into his face, piercings and all, and was suddenly overwhelmed with the realization that Jesus loved him so very much. I began to pray for him. I prayed for Christ to heal his brokenness. I prayed that his heart would be opened to the life-altering truth of God's love. I was so aware of this intense need to pray as the Holy Spirit directed me that I would not have been surprised to see Jesus suddenly appear beside him and lay His hand on the young man's shoulder. He got off a few stops later, but I know that in that moment I was given the privilege of entering into the passion of Christ to be known by that young man.

Living in the tension between the NOW and the SOMEDAY, the groaning and the glory, not only gives us a different perspective of this world, it also gives us a deeper sense of the hope we have that someday we will see Jesus face-to-face.

But as beautiful as heaven will be, it will be the presence of the One who loved us and gave Himself for us that will instantly erase all the sorrows, all the unfulfilled longings, all the broken dreams, all the unanswered questions, all the heartaches and pain. All of these things will simply be gone in the light and brilliance of heaven.

The Bible says that the tears that are still left will be brushed from our eyes by God Himself. He won't just say

"Stop crying!" Somehow there will be a personal dimension to our welcome home; our Father Himself will gather us into His embrace and we will be in His presence for all eternity. The groaning will be swallowed up in glory and the *someday* will be forever NOW.

AN INVITATION

Irene was a dear friend of my mother's. She was tiny and full of life. She would laugh and dance around her one-room apartment at the Mission where she worked, singing a song or telling us a funny story. She had very fine blonde hair that curled all over and thick Coke-bottle glasses. And she was diabetic. That's what finally took her from us when she was in her early forties.

I loved Irene. I loved her thick Scottish accent, her cherry pie with custard, and the way she loved me. She was a ray of sunshine in my lonely life. We would sometimes walk together, and she would quote poems and teach me hymns and challenge me to follow hard after God. In fact, when I read Paul's words in his letter to the Philippians, I can hear Irene's voice telling me, *"Everything else is worthless when compared with the priceless gain of knowing Christ Jesus, my Lord. I have discarded everything else, counting it all as garbage, so that I may have Christ and become one with Him"* (Philippians 3:8).

Irene's life was the story of her desire to know God. She was far from home, making very little money, serving behind the scenes as a secretary so others could do their jobs more efficiently. I remember her all these years later, and I wonder what motivated her to leave a comfortable life close to her family to pursue God in a foreign country.

I wonder what motivated the man in Matthew 13:45 to sell absolutely everything he had – chairs, tables, beds, pots, knickknacks, *everything,* to gain possession of one single pearl. And I wonder what he did when he finally got it.

It's hard to put a name to the passion that stirs inside a heart to answer the call to become still and know God, to stop trying to make it on our own, to take the provision that is offered, surrender to God's purposes, to accept His promise and learn to live in His presence. But I do know that although not everyone will be interested in coming along, the invitation is for everyone. It's not an exclusive club only for the very spiritual. It is a community of people committed to getting to know God together, not just when it's convenient or culturally expedient, but through the good times and the bad. Although this passion, this calling must be answered on an individual level, the journey is not meant to be taken alone. We do not learn to know God in a vacuum. We learn to know Him as we learn to love and care for others in His family.

If you look closely, you will see that this group is actually a community of broken people. We don't define ourselves by our brokenness; it doesn't become a badge of martyrdom, it just is a fact about us—one that gives us freedom to reach out to help others and to accept that same help when we need it.

In one of my seminary classes the instructor asked us to sketch a picture that represented how we felt about our various ministries. One young minister drew a picture of himself in front of his congregation. All the stick figures in his congregation stood straight and tall, but in his picture he stood before them leaning on crutches. The instructor looked at the picture, was silent for a moment, and then said, "You only need to change one thing: draw crutches for everyone." And that is the truth: we're broken people who know where to go to find wholeness.

This community of people longing to know God will not be a large group. Those who have traveled the farthest will tell you the greatest delights are found in being able to share your stories of grace and mercy and forgiveness and to hear the stories of others who know from experience what you're talking about. And so the writer to the Hebrews encourages us with these words:

> *Therefore, since we are surrounded by such a huge crowd of witnesses to the life of faith, let us strip off every weight that slows us down, especially the sin that so easily hinders our progress. And let us run with endurance the race that God has set before us.* ***We do this by keeping our eyes on Jesus, on whom our faith depends from start to finish.***
>
> Hebrews 12:1-2 (emphasis added)

The whole Bible is an invitation to "Be still and know that I am God." It is the story of men and women who found that invitation irresistible, and it's an amazing record of the faithfulness of the One who called them.

The invitation still stands, the adventure still waits, and the God who calls is still faithful.

Endnotes

Dedication

1. *The Pursuit of God*, A.W. Tozer, (Used by permission of WingSpread Publishers, a division of Zur Ltd., copyright © 1948, 1982, 1993 by Zur Ltd.), 9.

Chapter One

1. *The Pursuit of God*, A.W. Tozer, (Used by permission of WingSpread Publishers, a division of Zur Ltd., copyright © 1948, 1982, 1993 by Zur Ltd.), 65.

Chapter Two

1. *We Would See Jesus*, Roy and Revel Hession (Fort Washington, PA: Christian Literature Crusade, 1958), 23.
2. Augusta Dwyer, "Playing With Radiation," *MacLeans*, 2 Nov 1987.
3. *We Would See Jesus*, Roy and Revel Hession, 40.
4. *Ibid.* 40
5. *Ibid.* 41

Chapter Three

1. *Prayer: Finding the Heart's True Home,* Richard Foster (New York: HarperOne, 1992), 52.
2. Ibid., 53.
3. "Did Christ Die for Us or for God?" By John Piper. © Desiring God. Website: desiringGod.org

4. *My Utmost for His Highest*, Oswald Chambers (Grand Rapids, MI: Discovery House Publishers, l935 Dodd Mead & Co., renewed 1963 by the Oswald Chambers Publications Assn.,Ltd.), Sept. 13
5. *Mountain Breezes: The Collected Poems of Amy Carmichael*, Amy Carmichael (Fort Washington, PA: Christian Literature Crusade, 1999), 186
6. *My Utmost for His Highest*, Oswald Chambers (Grand Rapids, MI: Discovery House Publishers, l935 Dodd Mead & Co., renewed 1963 by the Oswald Chambers Publications Assn.,Ltd.), Sept 13
7. "Spirit of God, Descend Upon My Heart" (London: 1854, Text: George Croly, 1780-1860
Music: Frederick C. Atkinson, 1841-1897)
8. *Prayer: Finding the Heart's True Home*, Richard Foster (New York: HarperOne, 1992), 50.
9. Ibid., 56.
10. *My Utmost for His Highest*, Oswald Chambers (Grand Rapids, MI: Discovery House Publishers, l935 Dodd Mead & Co., renewed 1963 by the Oswald Chambers Publications Assn.,Ltd.), Dec. 9
11. *Devotional Classics: Selected Readings*, Richard Foster and James Bryan Smith, editors (New York, NY: HarperCollins Publishers, 1990, 1991, 1993 Renovare, Inc.), 266.
12. The life of Helen Roseveare has been documented by many. Her own books include: *Give Me This Mountain*, and *He Gave Us a Valley* (Fearn, Scotland: Christian Focus Publications, 2006).
13. *Mountain Breezes: The Collected Poems of Amy Carmichael*, Amy Carmichael (Fort Washington, PA: Christian Literature Crusade, 1999), 215

Chapter Four

1. *Celebration of Discipline*, Richard Foster (San Francisco: HarperSanFrancisco, 1988), 102.
2. *The Healing Path*, Dan B. Allender (Colorado Springs: WaterBrook Press; 1st edition, 1999), 21.
3. Alison Smith, "After God Left," *Real Simple*, Feb. 2008, page 65.
4. *The Complete Poetical Works of John Greenleaf Whittier*, by John Greenleaf Whitter (Boston: Houghton Mifflin Company, 1904)
5. *My Utmost for His Highest*, Oswald Chambers (Grand Rapids, MI: Discovery House Publishers, l935 Dodd Mead & Co., renewed 1963 by the Oswald Chambers Publications Assn.,Ltd.), October 30.
6. *The Holy Wild*, Mark Buchanan (Sisters, OR: Multnomah, 2003), 43.

7. *Fresh Wind, Fresh Fire,* Jim Cymbala (Grand Rapids: Zondervan, 1998), 19.
8. *Prayer: Finding the Heart's True Home,* Richard Foster (New York: HarperOne, 1992), 223.
9. *The North Face of God,* Ken Gire (Carol Stream, IL: Tyndale House, 2006), 98.
10. *George Muller of Bristol,* Arthur Pierson (Charlotte, NC: Baker and Taylor Co., 1899)

Chapter Five

1. As quoted by Mark Buchanan in *Things Unseen,* Mark Buchanan (Sisters, OR: Multnomah, 2006), 29.
2. *George Muller of Bristol,* Arthur Pierson (Charlotte, NC: Baker and Taylor Co., 1899) 32 (Fifty-Fifth Report)
3. *Where Is God When It Hurts?* Philip Yancey (Grand Rapids: Zondervan, 1977), 42
4. *Ruthless Trust,* Brennan Manning (New York: HarperCollins, 2002), 178.
5. Ibid., 150